Love, Fear

10 Love Letters
to Fear

Ebony White

This book is dedicated to:

MY GOD
My everything that I'm nothing without

MY HUSBAND, ABRAHAM
My love, encouragement, support, and all

MY DAUGHTERS, ABRIANA, NYAIZSHA, & ANYA
My "whys"

MY PARENTS, LARRY & YVONNE
My first people who loved me

Table of Contents

1 Chronicles 28:8

"Now therefore, in the sight of all Israel, the assembly of the Lord, and in the hearing of our God, be careful to seek out all the commandments of the Lord your God, that you may possess this good land, and leave it as an inheritance for your children after you forever."

INTRODUCTION

Fear is said to be one of the biggest dream killers. Do you agree, or do you just think it is one of those normal emotions that we all have to prove that we are only human? If that is your view, then I want you to stick with me through this book to adjust your perspective a little bit. You see, this book exposes how fear manipulates us from fulfilling our purpose. It highlights some of the mistakes I have made due to fear and its subtle power. It took time for me to realize that the main culprit in most of my adversities was fear, leading me to disobedience. Truth is, we must die to the flesh where fear resides, allowing no room for it to grow in our hearts.

This book gives examples of how I and many others have accepted the false emotions that put a hold on the manifestation of God's plan in our lives. These emotions appear real as we allow them to be implanted in our mind set, creating a facade of ourselves that is foreign to the demands of God. The enemy wants to do all he can to steal, kill, and destroy you, your purpose, your traditional legacy, and most importantly, your spiritual legacy.

During my enlightenment, God showed me how *Fear* simply used the Ten Commandments. Strategically, fear shields us from being obedient to our life rules, that is, God's commandments.

We consciously and unconsciously allow fear to execute its plan to hinder us from fulfilling God's will.

Friend, it is a battle of strategy against strategy, and you have to employ a spiritual strategy from God's word to defeat the scheme of fear. Too often, we give fear the freedom to reign in our heart, mind, and soul when we should give that freedom to God.

The 10 Love Letters from Fear expose the false perceptions fear provokes us to believe in any situation. We can also have false emotions that fear gives us toward people during moments of insecurity, depression, adversity, lack, and brokenness. We know and say what we should, but inside, we feel or act in a way we should not.

Each of us at some point, must develop the courage to defeat and overcome our fears if we yearn to make the most of our lives and fulfill our purpose. So, are you eager to journey with me on an adventure to RISE, REVIVE, and RELEASE from fear? Let us get started!

Chapter 1

GOD IS my one & only
(You shall have no other gods before me)

Dear Ebony,

I see that you have finally found your soul mate. Abraham appears to be a great guy, but do you think you can stand to watch and support him through this disease? I mean, you have never had to provide support for a loved one on this level. So, what makes you think you are designed for that kind of trauma?

In truth, stronger women have given up on their partners when faced with the reality of playing a nurse for the rest of their lives. Abe might have been the guy of your dreams, but now that he is sick, does he still fit into the future you dreamed of? Isn't harder to stand by and watch, especially as his wife? It hurts more even though you are not going through it. When you love someone, you tend to feel all their pain and yours at the same time. If he does not, I sure appreciate you. You have been a strong woman.

Besides, no matter how much you desire to help a loved one who is sick, your power is limited. You cannot do anything but support them the best way you know how to, which can be draining. I do not want to see you exhaust yourself this way in a bid to make someone happy. I just want to see your beautiful smile and the happy spark in your eyes. No one will blame you for not being strong enough to go through the illness with him. The truth is, you have the kids to take care of, and you need your sanity. It sucks when life takes the most important things out of your control.

Now, people will probably tell you to reach out in faith to a higher power. They say to pray, but that seems pointless, doesn't it? Why tell the "Big Man" up there what He already knows? God is supposedly watching you go through all this when He could change the situation miraculously. Mr. "All Powerful" could probably put up His pinky finger and change the scene, but apparently not; He seems to have His hand on His chin, watching you go through these challenges alone. Or perhaps, it is hard for Him to stand by and watch. Is He there for you like I am? This should make Him want to do something! It is almost like He's allowing your faith to be stripped away even though He says he'll never leave or forsake you.

I told **Doubt** all about this, and he is happy to hang with you through this. You at least have me, always choosing you. I commend you, my love, for sticking with Abe this far. But if it becomes too much, it is okay to throw in the towel. You have already done so much and proved that you are one of a kind. Abe even told you as his fiancé, "You did not sign up for this!"

You see, sometimes, things become harder than you expected because there is a possibility that it's not meant to be. I know you are holding in there because you want to be committed, loyal, and don't want him left alone in this. Even when God is absent, your loyalty and sense of responsibility make me want to be with you more and more.

God has not shown up, so do what you do. I will be here to comfort you, shield you from those who pretend to care, those who out-rightly do not care, and those just standing by spectating. I cannot bear the thought of you going through this alone or with people who still make you feel alone when they are around. So, let us just stick together, and I will never let you go! I know that you are happy with Abraham, but I am even happier with finding you!

Love, Fear'

New Love, New Pain

13

Have you ever had to fight a battle you didn't prepare for? I mean, even the greatest warriors must strategize before facing their opponents. But what if your adversary had the advantage of surprise? What if you were launched into a prolonged war you didn't see coming? How could you win such a battle?

When I met the man of my life and fell head over heels in love, I didn't see the pain in our future together. In fact, there were no obstacles, only happily ever after and lots of laughter. But it didn't turn out that way. Instead, I was thrown into a battle I didn't know I had the strength to fight.

Although, I didn't even know that this battle was a process I needed to go through at the time. Likewise, during those seasons, I had to fight for the life I wanted; I made a mistake by fighting alone. I listened to the voice of fear and turned my back on the only person who could have helped me – God.

I let every kind of emotion take the place of faith in my heart. Where God was supposed to guide me, I let fear lead the way. It's like the story of the Israelites who God rescued from Egypt. God wanted to lead them through the wilderness for forty days. But they listened to complaints and doubts, while led through the wilderness for forty years.

Looking back on what I experienced, I think I might have prolonged my journey to happiness and stability by listening to the wrong voices. I allowed fear to tell me that God abandoned me and didn't care about my family. I let doubt make me laugh in the face of God's promises and shut Him out of my life completely. But despite my faithlessness, I wasn't completely alone. I still saw showers and trickles of God's grace and mercy.

In the years I fought for the happiness I had found, I didn't just shut God out, but I also turned away from some people who sincerely cared. Yet, I wasn't experienced enough to know that fear was trying to isolate and destroy me. I thought it protected me from the pain of what I was going through. Rather than run towards God in times of trouble as the Bible teaches, I ran in the opposite direction. Ignoring my limitations, I silently vowed to sail through the stormy waves in my life and make it to shore without God's help or people.

Along the way, I learned valuable lessons that changed my life forever. Yet, it took me a long time before I had come to this conclusion. Unlike Job, who worshipped God immediately, he heard about the loss of his properties and the deaths of his children.

However, there's something worse than the death of a loved one. Death is final; afterward, there's a mourning process, and then you recover and get back to your life. But what about waking up every morning, not knowing if that day could be the last day you would spend with your husband? Think about that. It reminds me of one of those movies where the person goes to sleep and dreams about the same thing over and over. It's to the point that you can predict the day, but I didn't want to tell anyone, which gives room for it to happen. You know, what you think or say can bring it to fruition. For years, I woke up with the fear of losing my husband to a horrible sickness that wouldn't let him go. One moment, he was the man I fell in love with, full of life, and optimistic about the future. And the next, he was sick and fighting for his life.

Fear tried to get me to normalize seeing him in the hospital, tubes protruding from his body, helping him preserve his life. Was this battle about him, me, or both of us? Thing about that is, this was a battle none of us had signed up for willingly. Yet, I wasn't a deserter. My love was too genuine to give way under the pressure of a deadly illness. Even before we said our marriage vows, my love for Abe had been for better or worse. I was ready to laugh and cry with him. Yes, I was willing to suffer as well as enjoy happiness. However, if I had gotten a heads-up, it would have made things easier.

Why didn't God warn us? Why didn't He give us a sign? Most importantly, why was He so distant when we needed Him the most? Eventually, suffering hardened me towards God. I stopped asking for help or depending on Him for a miracle. Gradually, I grew to believe in my own ability. This would have been a good thing if it sprung from faith in God, but it was a false sense of self-sufficiency.

The truth is, no human being is self-sufficient. You need everyone God has brought into your life; they form your life support in challenging times. Much more, you need God, who is the only source of sufficiency.

So, join me on my journey as you discover all the things I had to go through and what happened along the way to becoming fearless in situations but fearful and adoring of God. Let's start from the beginning, right before Abe and I became husband and wife.

I Didn't See It Coming

My husband and I met in May of 2011 and got married on paper in November of 2012. Two days before that, Abraham, my husband had been discharged from the hospital after a 30-day stay where he was initially hospitalized due to an asthma attack at work.

I did not wake up that day knowing that it would affect my life the way it did. Who is ever prepared for a terrible life-changing situation? I mean, who wakes up with the thought, "All hell is going to break loose today, and my happiness will vanish."

Well, the same way no one prepares for these things, Abe's attack came as a shock. He was taken by ambulance from work, and then he was taken to the hospital. Before the incident, I had never been around someone during a full-blown asthma attack. I can't describe the emotions I experienced that day. One moment I was scared; the next, I would pray, and the next, I was wondering why and what is happening.

The asthma attack got so bad that he was put on a ventilator in an induced coma. But at that time, I was only his fiancé, not his wife. Sincerely, I never realized what being a fiancé in those circumstances meant. Being a fiancé during an emergency can be the most painful position for HIPAA hospital regulations and policies. There are more disadvantages than advantages. You are treated as a stranger to this person. You are on ice until you and your partner have chosen to get married and become one.

When you're a fiancé, it hurts, as though you are straddling the fence of wanting the best, making sure your fiancé is taken care of and treated well. At the same time, you are no more important than anyone else when it came down to it. The decision to put him into an induced coma was portrayed as though it was the doctors' decision, even though they consulted me first because this was fairly new to his medical history there.

I was the one there; my husband is from Texas. The only bloodline family here in Michigan is his daughter. I was put out of the hospital room in the ER once they began to intubate him. I did not know what to do at all because I had never been through such. My family didn't have any history of illnesses. My parents are in good health. Hell, I was in good health, and my nine-year-old daughter was too. Those 45 minutes in the waiting room for the doctor to report back felt like two to three hours. The doctor came in to let me know that he was under anesthesia. They had his levels stabilized to ensure that he would get some rest due to his body fighting to breathe correctly.

When I walked into the room, there were cords everywhere! Again, nothing I've ever seen before. The machine pumped and filled his body with air, breathing for him; his body depended on this machine for rest. I walked up closer to him, and I could see a tear in the corner of his eye and the salty residue left on the sides of his face from dried tears.

It hurt so badly because I did not know the level of pain and struggle he was experiencing. I grabbed his limp hand—that could not grab me back—to pray again, but I couldn't. All that I could say was, "God help him." Even though the doctors worked hard to save him, a part of me knew it was out of their hands. I needed someone more powerful and resourceful to intervene. I think that's why I uttered that quiet prayer.

I wiped the tear from the corner of his eye, wondering what he went through during the intubation. Was he scared, frustrated, weak, confused, or panicking? Either one frightened me to think that this was supposed to happen to him. I couldn't see that any good would come out of someone enduring suffocation. People are there to help, but they couldn't stop the attack while he was conscious. It's like drowning in a swimming pool and the tip of your finger just barely reaching the side of the pool to pull yourself out.

Everyone in the room watched Abe struggle for his life, but no one knew what was going on in his soul. What thoughts were going through his mind? Was his life flashing before him? Was he seeing a brilliant light? Or maybe he was approaching heaven's pearly gates? I hated seeing him like that; so pale and drained. He was the one who was drowning and didn't have the power to save himself.

Most people think that love only heals wounds and soothes pain. Well, it does, but it also causes pain. It was hard for me to experience Abe's suffering because I loved him so much and was willing to do anything for him. Love for him made it harder for me. The doctors care, but most times they don't have an emotional attachment to their patients. They didn't feel like someone was ripping out their heart on the table. Neither did they see their future slowly slipping away from them like the sun at the end of the day. At that moment, nothing was too great a price to pay for Abe's recovery. But I could not do anything to help him.

After that day, he was in a coma for about two and a half days. One thing I'm grateful for is the fact that he didn't remain in the coma. I literally would go to the hospital and sit with him for at least 2 hours at a time. I tried to get a break or get things done in between because I still had a daughter at home. Fortunately, my mother helped me take care of her. As I remember those trying times, I thank God for her, especially in those moments I had to be at the hospital with Abe. With the love and understanding from my mother, I didn't have to worry about my daughter. Abe was enough to worry about at the time.

The Trouble with Being Abe's Fiancé

During the next week and a half later, his health was still unstable. Occasionally, he would have difficulty breathing at the most unexpected times. No one could understand why or how his levels were normal, but he was having these issues breathing. Most importantly, there was no drastic decrease in oxygen.

One day I came up to the hospital after work, and he was sitting in his recliner in the hospital room. He wanted to go for a walk, so we did. After that, we came back into the room. He sat on the bench, not wanting to sit in the same spot he had been in for a while. So, I sat in the recliner with my feet up. An hour later, the nurse came in to give him medicine, which may have contained about two to three narcotics for pain and cough.

While he took his meds, I reminisced about when I was a certified nursing assistant. Anytime we gave meds to a resident, we needed to put them to bed first. Why? Because most narcotics made the patients drowsy and getting them in bed alleviated fall risks. So, after Abe had taken the meds, I asked him if he wanted to go to bed because he looked like he was getting tired. He chose to sit up for a little while longer to continue talking to me about his day. I asked him again if he wanted to go to bed, and he said yes, so he stood up and began leaning to his right. Before I could stand up and help him, he had fainted on his side in the doorway, sliding into the hallway. I could not believe what had just happened. I screamed for the nurse; she came down to ensure he was coherent, and then more nurses came. He was examined, and we discovered that his neck had broken in three spots. When I tell you Abraham does things big, you've got to believe me. He needed emergency surgery, so again the doctors had to decide for him because I was only his fiancé.

After he had surgery, he began to have a few more flare-ups with his asthma all over again. Now he had two things to heal from: asthma attacks and a broken neck. A week later, he was still admitted to the hospital. During my lunch, I went to see him, and the nurse reported to me that he had fallen. I went into his room to talk to him about it. Before Abraham fell and broke his neck, he was never considered a fall risk. Therefore, he did not have on gripper socks that were red in color to indicate to the hospital staff that this patient needed assistance in moving around, getting up, and couldn't perform simple tasks alone. So, because there was no indication, Abe chose to get up and put himself in his chair, unaware that he was supposed to ask for assistance, and he fell.

Now mind you, he had been on a pain pump for days. At this point, I had to show my "default setting," as Sarah Jakes calls it. I wanted the hospital staff to treat him well and not neglect him. He had been through a lot already, and it appeared as though no one took him or his situation seriously anymore. I had spoken with two nurse managers about the service and what I perceived as negligence in his plan of care.

23

After that point, any information that I wanted or asked about was vaguely answered. I didn't know why. It came to a head that as Abe's fiancé, I had stayed at his side for the past three weeks, yet the hospital no longer needed me for information. They did not like that I was very inquisitive, caring, and particular about his well- being. I needed to understand why or what was being given or done to him. Instead of me any longer, they decided to require a "next of kin" authorize that information can be given before they could discuss Abe's health with me. The closest person that lived in Michigan at one point was one of his nieces, who was old enough to give consent. I couldn't believe how the hospital had used me to gain as much information as they wanted, and then when I needed information, they didn't want to give it to me.

It hurt me so much that I was treated this way just for standing by the side of the person I love. I realized that when the hospital had needed someone to provide care and comfort for him, they had just put up with me. The hospital didn't value my relationship with Abe because it wasn't binding and required things to be explained. Perhaps, they expected and wanted me to leave him and carry on with my life.

Anyway, I can't blame them for their assumptions because they had seen such cases countless times. Women whose fiancés become unexpectedly ill break off their engagements after considering the burden of living in uncharted predicaments. In fact, married couples have been known to get divorced over prolonged or unexpected illnesses. So, an ordinary engagement that didn't legally commit me to be responsible for Abraham wasn't enough for the hospital. I could only be taken somewhat serious as his wife.

Well, there was little I could do except request a patient advocate. I did just that, she suggested that we have a power of attorney done. We completed the paperwork, but there are always loopholes in everything.

But the next morning, while I was at work, I received an incredible idea that changed things for Abe and myself. One of my coworkers and friend had asked how Abe and I were doing. At that moment, I felt overwhelmed by all the pent-up emotions. I broke down in tears; it was then that I hadn't realized how Abe's illness and the treatment from the hospital had gotten to me. I have never felt so belittled to my face. Do you know what it means to be shut out? First, I had no power to help Abe beyond providing my love and support. Now, even that was taken away from me because the doctors won't talk to me. I had told her what had happened the evening prior, and she suggested that we just go ahead and get married, do something small and intimate just to at least have it down on paper if this happened again.

We did not leave the hospital with the assurance that it wouldn't happen again, so that didn't appear to be a bad idea. The only thing that I was concerned about was the moment of walking down the aisle. This is the first and only time I will be getting married. I wanted nothing to destroy the moment. Thinking over the conversation I had with the patient advocate and nurse, it's only an issue being his fiancé, not his wife, so I took that suggestion back to Abraham.

I thought he would say the same he did, but he always had a positive outlook on things in hard times than me. He agreed to get married in a small way and said, "Nothing will take away from July 13, 2013 unless you allow it to. You will be in your wedding dress, on a beach, white sand between your toes, right in front of the ocean. You will have your bridesmaids and groomsmen, pink rose petals everywhere, and me standing at the altar in the suit that you picked out for me. Everything will happen just the way you've planned it for the last year. There is nothing more special than your dream happening right before your eyes. That moment will not and cannot be taken from you. We will do this only to protect ourselves, regardless of what anyone thinks, and we will still have our day. No one will need to know unless we tell them."

So, we organized an intimate wedding at our church with no more than ten people. That moment made me even more excited for July 13th. Between November 2012 and July 13th, we were in and out of the hospital because of Abe's asthma attacks at least two more times. Evidently, the move we made was a wise one. We got married in Cocoa Beach, Florida, just as planned, went on our honeymoon, and had our hometown reception. Absolutely nothing was taken away from that moment for us!

It's incredible that we could still have such a magical experience amid all the challenges with Abe's health and how I was treated at the hospital. But you see, there's always a way around the problems that threaten to steal your happiness. A way is, God! In myself and Abe's case, his asthma almost robbed us of our future happiness, but we didn't allow it to. I'm so grateful for Abe's positive disposition. Even though he was the one sick, he could cheer me out of my despair and make me see that our happiness couldn't be taken from us unless we leave the door open for it to happen.

Years of Struggle

Have you noticed that life doesn't show you a part of itself and leave out the rest? It shows you bitterness and sweetness, ugliness and beauty, pain and bliss. Abe and I had our fairytale marriage, we got to be together despite the obstacles, yet life found a way to bring in the negative side again.

Fast-forwarding to the year of 2018, Abraham's asthma visits to the hospital began to increase again. There may have been one visit every couple of months, but the year 2019 was when it really hit hard. We had been in the hospital at least once a month, with hospital admissions being at least one week every time. When the frequency began to increase, I had not realized from 2013 to 2018 how much I had relied on my husband. In 2015, we had a baby together. We went through our five-year struggles, but we continued to move forward, knowing we were meant to be.

Abe and I worked at the same place, in the same position, on the same floor, and about four rows apart. Every time he had an asthma attack at work, I would either have to take him to the hospital or if it was really bad, he would need to be taken by ambulance. It began to happen so often at work that we got scared he'd lose his job. His annual leave, sick leave, and FMLA was running out. Even my leave balance at work was affected because I mainly cared for him.

Also, I noticed a pattern of him having these attacks at work more and more often; even through the years, it had me questioning the environment we worked in. I still believed in God's existence and his ability to heal Abe, but it was hard to sit back and watch this all play out. I wanted to continue trusting it'll work out for our good again.

My trust in God became fainter and fainter every time we went to the hospital that year. My anger began to fester inside me towards God for allowing all this to happen to my husband again. He wouldn't take control of this asthma that had taken over our lives, hope, and joy. Wasn't His love supposed to show us compassion? Didn't He heal people because He loved them and didn't want to see them hurt? Then why was our case any different? A lot of questions rushed through my mind, and many of them remained unanswered. I didn't know that I was nurturing a mild resentment towards God.

You would think that only Abraham suffered physically, but I suffered physically, emotionally, and mentally as his wife. My body would ache all over, but I still had to be strong or appear to be at least because I was not the one in physical pain. I had to appear strong to my children, family, friends, and associates. Also, I had to appear strong to people we didn't know to avoid pity. During the periods of the attacks, I allowed fear to take over my mind about people, their good intentions, genuine concern, as well as God.

The fear came from the fact that every morning we woke up together, took our children to school, and headed to work, there was a possibility that he may not return home with us that day. That's how frequent this was. My whole demeanor and attitude changed while he was not home and hospitalized. My patience became thinner and thinner with my children, and I expected them to somewhat sympathize with me as much as I did for them.

But I was tripping at that time; I had a four-year-old and a sixteen-year-old in the house with me. Those are perfect ages for displaying "it's all about me," and rightfully so. I did not look to Abraham because of what he was going through himself. In my mind, I had never felt so alone in my life. Even though it happened too often, I still felt alone while he was home because I decided to keep it all in, not to stress him out. At the same time, I became vexed with this part of my life and with people.

I began to pay attention to the fact that these attacks were more stimulated at work. I shared with Abe that if he were ever able to return to work, that he would need to work from home or elsewhere. It doesn't help that the building was old. We don't know what's in the air. Even our older daughters would tell him he needed to get out of there, and that's where it was coming from. Our coworkers would tell him the same thing, but he did not know how terrified I was about this. At least a few times a week, when he was well enough to go back to work, I contemplated about not wanting to become a widow. I loved him too much to lose him. I lost my independence to become dependent on him, and now to jump into the role of that I-N-D-E-P-E-N-D-E-N-T woman again, was hard for me. It was like starting all over, mentally, resetting my mind to adjust to the spontaneous circumstances.

Listening to Fear

Each time, I would cry myself to sleep the initial night he was admitted because I would be in a funk and not as nice as I could have been to my children. It was the stress I was enduring, and the level of fear that built up into anger. I knew their dad's illness was hard on them too, but sometimes I couldn't help it. Yes, I still had vulnerable moments where I cried on someone's shoulder here and there, but then fear would speak to me, telling me that I should not have told them about it or cried in their presence.

They don't care about one word you just said once you depart from them. They are going about their lives and don't care about

31

yours. People had been commending you on how strong you are and look at you, crying. THEY DON'T CARE ABOUT YOU! God doesn't care about you! They will always ask how he is doing, not you. Look, they don't help with anything; they just get to see that you aren't what they thought you were. Dry that cry baby stuff up and tell people to stay out of your business if they aren't doing anything past being nosey.

Funnily enough, I listened to this voice. Even though it turned me against people who genuinely cared and isolated me in my pain, it provided the kind of defense I thought that I needed. I didn't want to be vulnerable and dependent on others. Hell, I didn't want them to see my family as some charity case. Therefore, I fell for that voice in my head that appeared to care. But fear was out to destroy what was left of my happiness. The voice kept echoing in my head and hardening my heart towards everyone around me. After so long, I went with it.

I changed my vulnerability to an attitude, kept to myself, cut out of church, worked two jobs, and cried at night. Sometimes I was too tired to cry at night. My day consisted of getting kids to school, get myself to work, go to the hospital on lunch if I didn't have something else that needed to be done, go to the hospital after work, and head to my second *gig* if I had appointments. Every day I had to pick up the kids from my mom. I always felt obligated to go to the hospital because I didn't trust the care of the doctors, nurses, or aides until I met them and felt their vibe.

Listening to the voice of fear damaged my trust in God. Can you imagine going through something so painful without God? I was so angry at the hand I was dealt, and I blamed everything on God. At first, it felt like God was indifferent and didn't care what happened to my family and me. But then, fear made me feel like God was orchestrating every evil occurrence and torment we were going through. So, I started seeing the situations in my life as punishment from God.

I thought that God had placed so much on me that he wasn't allowing me to get a breath in. He was farthest from my thoughts. I had to keep this family afloat on my own, God may show his face at some point, but he better not take my husband from me. He is the love of my life; he supposedly gave him to me and now we are in this rut. Our youngest daughter has moments where she realizes she hasn't seen him in a while and has this burst of tears come at any given time.

Something about the Building

In the middle of 2019, the director of our work building had requested that an air quality test needed to be done on the building's second and maybe third floor. A few other workers were having breathing/ asthma issues as well. Abe just happened to be the worst case that would end up in the hospital. About a month later, we got an email saying that the levels were "normal" in the building. LOL, normal for who? That is trash! Abe, of course, recovered at home and was well enough to return to work.

The day he returned to work in June, he had discovered some weird things about his workstation. He inquired about them, but the truth was not in sight. He continued to unpack the lies from the bag they were giving him out from their mouths, which led to an unforeseen incident. About 30 minutes later, he went into a full-blown asthma attack. After he had just been home for at least three weeks with no issues. That was the turning point for me, I was drowning in fear and anger. Fear that this has happened too many times, and at some point, his body is going to give in to what's at hand or he is going to give in from being tired of this.

I was angry because no one seemed to care enough to get to the bottom of it. This was 100 percent up to me, from my "self-sufficient" standpoint. I also had to comfort him with the building director and assistant right there, witnessing what happens to him during these occurrences. I was also assuring myself in my head that this would be the last day he would step foot in that building.

It took me back to the very first time I experienced this with him in 2012. We got married so that I could act on his behalf and protect him with anything within my reach. I received text messages of prayers and concerns from coworkers stating clear as day that it is something in the building. This is what I had already known. I took it upon myself to request a meeting with the director to see what her next step was because some action needed to be taken. This also made me question the type of people we work under and for. Especially in these bigger companies, corporate, and government entities but that's another subject in itself. The next morning, I had a meeting with the director and two other managers. It was basically a fact-finding meeting. They wanted to play as if they don't see what I see, plus I wanted to look them in their eye as they mentally gathered their choice of words to give to me. The woman who loves her husband with all she has and knows to give. A woman who has been by her husband's side since day one. A woman who has had to watch her husband suffer from something that had taken a sudden turn in damaging and affecting his health, life, family, mental stability, physical ability, sometimes his spirituality, but definitely his wife's faith and trust in God. A woman who is not only angry but fearful that one day she could have to bury her husband because of this.

I was fearful that this could really happen, if I were not forceful enough on her about my husband asking for a change in the location of his position or even quit. How could I live with myself after that? Knowing that I could have saved him if I would have pushed a little more. I would have to look into our children's eyes, knowing I did not give my all to his fight. To add injury to insult, all three managers were women. Two out of the three were married. I dazed off while watching their lips move, saying there wasn't much more that could be done, and he may run out of long-term disability if he does not return soon...

My insides felt like the stirring of a hurricane. I could not bear this any longer so I just blurted out, "This is my husband, and he will not step foot in this building until we know what is causing this! What about the air quality test you did?" Consider the implications of the words I had uttered. I had gotten to a point where I no longer cared how we'd survive if Abe didn't have his job. Instead, I was more concerned about his life than anything else. I requested a copy of that report, wanting it that day. They looked at each other and said "yes". Boom, that should be a good start in finding out what's going on.

I go back to my desk and less than an hour later, I had the report in my hand. I skimmed through the first few pages of the report and seen several things that didn't look too good. I locked it in my drawer in my purse and took it home. It was put in a safe place.

A few days later, Abe was well enough for me to reveal the report to him. After he was released from the hospital, I instructed him to get an allergy test done to see if anything matches. By God's grace, he was able to slip in a cancellation spot. He comes to see me on my lunch to show me the results of his allergy test. We discovered that what he is severely allergic to is in the air and was in his cubicle. I could not believe the resemblance in the items on both reports, so much so, I almost said thank you, Jesus. I was so clouded with abandonment and blame toward God that I didn't say it. I knew that was only the beginning of what was to come. We received word that he had about a week and a half to return to work or his position would be terminated. I had emailed the director again to let her know that I had followed her specific suggestion on getting the allergy test done by who she told us to and that we have the results. How ironic that is? I took them up to her, made copies where I highlighted the specific similarities in both reports. She even had to buck her eyes and twist her neck at them. So, I asked again, what could be done about this being that his doctor is not releasing him to work in this building?

The doctors have pretty much exhausted all options and are now considering an experimental 3- part procedure. She stated to me that she could move him to a higher floor in the building and that it was not an option for a work from home position to be granted under the circumstances. I wanted to laugh in her face. They are doing our same position from home, the same type of information, and lying about being in their work area.

I have seen workers get moved around for no rhyme or reason at all, and you mean to tell me that his life is in danger in this building, and you can't propose that he work from home. I got up and just walked out, left the copies on her desk to allow her a moment alone to bathe in the fact that messed up and will eventually pay for this. Now mind you, he had worked there for over fifteen years, was one of the higher seniority workers in that position, and he could perform the work just not in this building. Moving him to another floor within the building does not guarantee me that this won't happen again here. If it is in the air, then it is everywhere, I explained.

I could see straight through her that the odds were against him. Was this the plan for getting rid of a worker who has not been disciplined or written up, been there for almost 2 decades, and was also the chief union steward? Now I'm wondering where is the help when he needs it? He has helped many people keep their jobs. He has helped deescalate many situations in that building between supervisors and staff. He has always been a worker that they knew and said would be a good manager but never promoted. There wasn't even any help given from the union he represented. Watching this happen to him, was hurting more and more. It brought me more resentment against the people directly and indirectly involved. Talk about being used and abused...

I began to build up hatred; no one can be trusted at this point. My husband is the type of man that needs to work to contribute to the household, and if he loses the job, he loses one of his sources of money. In which I didn't want them to be the cause of him feeling inadequate. They couldn't appreciate him or was intimidated by one of their best employees. By the time I got back to my desk, the director let me know that it was a HIPAA violation for her to keep his medical information, so I told her to dispose of it at her own discretion. She sent the assistant manager to my desk to drop it off. About a week later, he had been terminated. I was glad that by this point, I was able to show Abe that he had so much more to offer another company and this world. He is way more valuable than being stuck at a desk in an old building that was trying to kill him. It was no surprise to me that God had allowed this to happen. I had also taken a mental leave from this job after they had just fired my husband for being allergic to toxic particles in the air to the point that he had been put into 3 medically induced comas over time. His body built up an intolerance to it causing the asthma attacks, the building made him sick, and he gets fired.

Can you imagine the lack of empathy from a governmental entity where a person has been so loyal and faithful to for fifteen years can result in? There were no accommodations and try to tell me there aren't many options available when you have various work locations throughout the entire state. I could not grin and bear in the faces of selfishness, unreasonable, scheming, crookedness. Every time she smiled, it reminded me of the Cheshire cat from Alice in Wonderland. The mischievous look stirred up that hurricane inside every time. I knew it was time for me to leave so that I could leave without doing anything I would regret later for the loyalty and respect I have for my husband. Also, just for the fact that I knew I would probably be the next person they would intentionally try to terminate. I had done a lot of thinking during my leave of absence and took a position elsewhere. I refuse to work under and for people who outright show you that you mean nothing to them. It was best said by Maya Angelou, "when someone shows you who they are, believe them the first time. People know themselves much better than you do. That's why it's important to stop expecting them to be something other than who they are." This situation taught me that you should never dish out loyalty and faithfulness to anyone or anything more than you give to God. No one or nothing stands a chance against the undeniable love that God has for us. Fear wanted us to keep him in that job, in that building so that he could do his ultimate stealing, killing, and destroying. He also wanted us to depend on these jobs to supply our needs in a place where our purpose or potential was not appreciated. God had something bigger in mind for us and of more value. He is the only one who never fails at being who He says He is and what He says He'll do!

Chapter 2:

GOD IS my love
(You shall worship Me)

Dear Love,

Since we've been getting acquainted, I have a clearer view of what I need and want. It's you that fills my world. You have shown me how important I am to you. You always seem to need me. I love that you are so emotional and react to the trials that come your way when things don't go your way. We plan things out for a reason. But I guess "God" always has to have things His way too. He's so uncompromising of the time and thought we put into our planning.

For instance, remember when you called on me to get financing for another car you wanted? Even though your payment was higher, you still had me when you went to pay other bills. God could have gotten you that job you interviewed for to accommodate for the car note. But He didn't. I planned for that pay increase for you with *Materialistic*; now we must find you a job with compatible pay to it. This could help the family and bills.

So why would your husband not want you to get better any opportunity you can get? Who has time to be complacent? We got to grind day in and day out. Why can't he see that? You are a woman with dreams, and I want to see them come through for you. I'm not sure about him, though. You give me life. Baby, I always got your back! If it were up to me, your wish would be my command. I want to be your soft place, just like you are my soft place, soft as the silk sheets. I want to lay on in your mind, heart, and soul with you. Your pouting lips look sweet as honey when you say certain things that get you upset. Your fire lights my fire and keeps me going. I devote my life and my love to you.

Love, Fear

Seeking the Wrong Things

Ever since I bought my first car, I always wanted a new car every time something new came out. It was never a smaller car, or on the cheaper end, it had to be a full-size car. My legs were too long to fit in a compact car. It took me a long time to see the consequences of car hopping and paying the minimum on the car note instead of paying extra every month. All I knew is that I wanted that car and nothing else!

Looking back, I could have driven a little car like a two-seater, pushing the driver seat back as far as I could and leaning the seat back for more room. Not to mention, I was also living outside of my means. I was still living with my parents with my daughter. There were several cons to what *"Materialistic"* was doing in my small mindset. No, my car notes weren't as much as a rent payment for a decent place, but it could have allowed for me to save up to purchase a decent car to get me from point A to point B and a head start to move into my own place.

I think the fear of being alone as a teen mother crippled my level of determination to move out. I didn't even realize the debt I was putting myself into before I started a full life of my own. I had a rollover into a vehicle I needed a whooping for. The only pro to purchasing or financing a newer car is that it is less likely to turn right around and pay for car repairs. That's one thing I can say that I have not had much experience with all my years of driving. Once that rollover happened, I slowed down. But then it rolled over to wanting a new house.

I began t develop irritation for anything no longer wanted. The next thing I wanted to change was my job. But of course, I wanted a higher-paying job to pay for the higher costing new things I wanted. It began to always be about things. Until I realized, if we had a significant increase in income, then I could afford to do all these switch-ups if I wanted to.

I had this approach to life because I was seeking the wrong things. God is not against His children desiring good things and working hard, but He also wants our hearts to be in the right place. In my case, my heart was on material things that didn't matter much in God's plans and purposes.

Why don't they matter? Because God has promised to do the caring for us? He has promised to take care of our needs and make our satisfaction His priority. How do I know? Matthew

6:31-33 says, *"Therefore take no thought, saying, What shall we eat? or, What shall we drink? or, Wherewithal shall we be clothed? (For after all these things do the Gentiles seek:) for your heavenly Father knoweth that ye have need of all these things. But seek ye first the kingdom of God, and his righteousness; and all these things shall be added unto you."*

In the text above, Jesus teaches us to avoid worrying over earthly things. Understand that He didn't say they aren't important, but He spoke against letting them consume your heart. You can be so materialistic and conscious of your needs that all your life becomes about how you can make more money or pay bills. Such a life is slavery to this world, and God doesn't want that for us. Instead, God wants us to be confident in His ability to provide for our needs.

For this reason, Jesus teaches us that God knows all our needs. Certainly, if God knows your needs and loves you, then He's willing to supply those needs. So those years I was in pursuit of things, I ignored the Father's concern for me and His power to provide my needs limitlessly. I was seeking my kingdom. I had it all figured out; what I wanted my life and family to look like. What about God's kingdom and how He wanted my life to turn out? That wasn't in mind.

It took some time, but I eventually discovered that I was supposed to seek His kingdom and righteousness. All those things I pursued were supposed to follow me. Yes, they are my right as a devoted child of God. You might be where I was, but it's not too late. Today, you can stop seeking the wrong things. God doesn't want you to dedicate your whole life to paying bills and pursuing trends. He has made you for a greater purpose, and there's rest in seeking God's kingdom. But what is God's kingdom? It's the reign of His will and dominion in your heart and around your life. The things you seek will influence your heart, just like the things I sought influenced my heart.

Humble Yourself Before God

Materialism has a way of filling your heart with pride and confidence. The more you achieve in the pursuit of your desires, the more confident you'll become in your ability. But the truth is, God doesn't want us to be confident in our abilities.

For instance, the Bible talks about a great and might king who was blessed by God. King Nebuchadnezzar had an enormous empire that encompassed most nations of the world. However, the Bible reveals that God gave him this dominion. Yet, the King didn't recognize God. You can see materialism in his words in Daniel 4:30 (KJV): *"The king spake, and said, Is not this great Babylon, that I have built for the house of the kingdom by the might of my power, and for the honour of my majesty?"*

You see, materialism is not just focusing on earthly possessions. It also includes the purpose behind your desire. In this text, King Nebuchadnezzar falsely bragged about building his impressive kingdom by his power. Then, he revealed that everything he did was for his glory and honor. Do you see that the king neither acknowledged God's help nor God's will; the kingdom was all about himself. Because of the king's pride and materialism, God humbled him, and for seven years, he was banished into the bush and ate grass like an animal.

You don't need to wait for God to humble you like this king. Is there any trace of materialism in your life? You can begin to deal with it today. Some of the signs to look out for are include discontentment with what you already have, unhealthy desire for material things, confidence in your abilities, and disregard for God's will. Searching your heart for these signs will prompt you to seek God's help and humble yourself before Him.

Gradually, God revealed the contents of my heart and led me to repentance. He even used my husband to change my perspective. One day my husband asked me, "Are you ever satisfied?" I initially felt insulted, wanting to clutch my pearls, outright appalled. But then I asked, what do you mean? He said, well, within the last two years, you have gotten a new home, a new job, and the car you wanted. Miraculously by God, we can even afford it all comfortably. Now, you are still running around here stressing yourself with ways and ideas on how to generate more money. You have not taken the time to soak in what blessings you have already received. I'm thinking who has time to settle, but at the same time, I see what he means.

Do you see the contrast between my husband's words and the words of King Nebuchadnezzar? My husband was pointing me to God. God has already blessed me so much and needed to acknowledge His goodness towards me. It was contrary to the voice in my head that told me I needed to do more to get more.

Materialism tells you that all you have is by your plans and achievement. It tells you that if you want to have more, you need to do more. But where does God fit in? The worst thing is, you lose your peace and joy over things that don't matter. Being materialistic makes us too busy and too agitated to appreciate what God has already done.

At some point, you need to give yourself time to soak in what's around you, just to make a comparison of where you were and where you are now. Occasionally, you need to take inventory of your blessings, especially the ones you know for a fact you didn't deserve. That's called humbling yourself before God. He should get the credit always but more so when we can see that we hung around those so-called friends like Materialistic. King David made this his daily practice; he thought about God's goodness towards him. Here are some of David's Psalms that will help you soak in God's blessings.

Psalm 8:3-9 will make you marvel at God's love and affection in your life.

"When I consider Your heavens, the work of Your fingers, The moon and the stars, which You have ordained, What is man that You are mindful of him, And the son of man that You visit him? For You have made him a little lower than the angels, And You have crowned him with glory and honor. You have made him to have dominion over the works of Your hands; You have put all things under his feet, All sheep and oxen— Even the beasts of the field, The birds of the air, And the fish of the sea That pass through the paths of the seas. O LORD, our Lord, How excellent is Your name in all the earth!"

Psalm 103:1-10 contains testimonies of God's goodness that you can relate to. Thinking upon them and saying them back to God will enable you to humble yourself before God;

"Bless the LORD, O my soul; And all that is within me, bless His holy name! Bless the LORD, O my soul, And forget not all His benefits: Who forgives all your iniquities, Who heals all your diseases, Who redeems your life from destruction, Who crowns you with lovingkindness and tender mercies, Who satisfies your mouth with good things, So that your youth is renewed like the eagle's. The LORD executes righteousness And justice for all who are oppressed. He made known His ways to Moses, His acts to the children of Israel. The LORD is merciful and gracious, Slow to anger, and abounding in mercy. He will not always strive with us, Nor will He keep His anger forever. He has not dealt with us according to our sins, Nor punished us according to our iniquities."

Occasionally, you need to take inventory of your blessings, especially the ones you know for a fact you didn't deserve. That's called humbling yourself before **God**.

Godliness and Contentment

What I'm about to say might be tough to accept, but it's the truth. God didn't call you to become the richest person earth. Neither were you saved to have everything you desire. Rather, God calls you to godliness and contentment. 1 Timothy 6:5-6 (NKJV) says, *"useless wranglings of men of corrupt minds and destitute of the truth, who suppose that godliness is a means of gain. From such withdraw yourself. Now godliness with contentment is great gain."* You shouldn't pressure yourself to fit into a stereotype or keep to trends. Although God promises to give us abundance, He wants us to live simple and moderate lives. God wants us to always be grateful for what we have, not covetous.

I'm not in competition with anyone except myself. But we are our biggest critic. I am very hard on myself, and that's the next thing my husband said. It even had gotten to the point where my attitude and actions made him feel as though he wasn't doing something right or enough, causing me to be dissatisfied and unhappy. He had done all he knew to do, plus more. I told him that I must deal with this, and it has nothing to do with you not being who and what I need.

After that, it took me to recognize that I saw money as the source, not a resource or tool. Yes, we would pay tithe and offerings, but eventually, I would catch myself in a regiment to receive more money from God. Later down the road, conviction came to show me what I was doing. I was gold-digging God! I began to fear that maybe it's not for me to be rich or "very comfortable financially" in this life. I dropped any extra dreams, side jobs, and aspirations I had.

Once I realized my mentality, I saw my convictions as a reason to punish myself once again. I tried for maybe a week to follow the wake-up, take kids to school, go to work, get off of work, pick up kids, and go home during those days. You know the American normalcy. It drove me insane not to look at real estate investment strategies, financial investments, knowledge on how the rich got rich... At that moment, I was lost, confused, and tired of not being on the path I felt I should be on to get ahead.

1 Corinthians 10:13 says, don't be common, be faithful; that is where temptation is. That Sunday, I went to church; things flowed as normal, gave tithes and offerings, and waited for the sermon. Well, then this turned into one of those Sundays that has its flow, nothing you can control about it. I'm like dang, right when I'm going through mentally, here we go. The tears were flowing, conviction hit, and the answer came.

During the service, Bishop asked for anyone wanting to start a business to stand. If you need someone to stand here and tell you that you can do it, stand. If you are serious, come to the altar. I stood and went to the altar. He laid hands on each one of us there, simply done. Of course, it had to be me to break the simplicity of this moment. There was more to be said than a prayer. He prophesied to me as my husband stood in the pulpit. Let's just say my life is nowhere near set to be normal in God's will.

There will be several businesses; we will need to take risks and be prepared because it's coming within the next five years. When I got that word from God through Bishop, I wrote every single word down that he said. It's something about when you put it on paper, but that's another discussion. That inspired me to research how we should look at money- as a tool.

Money is only a tool

From my research, I discovered that money is a tool. Most people worship money and see it as the answer to all their problems. But that's a wrong mindset. Instead, God is the answer to all of life's troubles. Psalm 50:15 (KJV) says, *"And call upon me in the day of trouble: I will deliver thee, and thou shalt glorify me."* You'll see in scriptures that God wants us to master this world's resources and use them for the kingdom.

Zechariah 1:17 (NKJV) says, *"Again proclaim, saying, 'Thus says the LORD of hosts: "My cities shall again spread out through prosperity; The LORD will again comfort Zion, And will again choose Jerusalem. "* God knows the importance of money to your life and His kingdom, it's a means to an end. But that's all it should be, a means. But unfortunately, so many people have made it the purpose of their lives. They just want more money and are willing to compromise their godly principles to get it. Others who haven't strayed so far still depend on money like it's their God.

Have you been there before? When you have money so you can be happy and motivated, but you're sad without it? God wants you to know that money is just a tool. Do you understand that? God has many tools, and money is one of them. Therefore, He can choose to supply all your needs by giving you more money, or He can provide using other means.

I want to use money for the freedom of my time and to fully focus on my purpose, everything else will be added. Think about what Zechariah 1:17 says. If God desires to advance His kingdom on earth through prosperity, then it means He'll prosper you. Yes, you don't have to fight or cut corners for it. All you have to do is pursue the reason for the prosperity- God's kingdom.

Doesn't it make sense that if you focused on what brings the money that God will supply it? You can change your mind set about money. In the past, you might have thought about a new car or a new dress whenever you thought about money, but today, be transformed. Anytime you think of money, think of the kingdom because money is a tool. A man of God once listed reasons God gave Him for being rich:

1. To be a blessing -You can't help the poor by being one of them

2. Speed and mobility - preaching the gospel to the ends of the earth as commanded by Jesus requires a lot of resources.

3. Time – When you're rich, you have a full supply, and money works for you. You don't need to spend all your time pursuing a salary; instead, you'll control your own time.

Did you notice that all these reasons are focused on God's kingdom? Believers should desire to prosper because they want to fulfill God's will for them. Therefore, prosperity is not the end. When you adopt God's vision and purpose, the way you use money will be refined. Before, I used money to satisfy my cravings and desires. Money gave me confidence and things I should depend on God for. In that sense, it wasn't a tool but a large part of my life. What kind of relationship do you have with money? Some people become obsessed with money that they become slaves. As a believer, you must remember that you're a pilgrim. You should be in pursuit of God's kingdom and willing to advance it with any tool He makes available.

How I Learnt About Stewardship

One day, Jesus taught His disciples about richness towards God. He wanted them to know that possessions didn't make on rich before God. To communicate effectively, He told them a story about a rich fool. What made this man a fool? Well, He was rich but didn't know why. Stewardship is simply understanding who owns the resources available to you and what to use them for. Let's take a look at what Jesus said in Luke 12: 15-21 (NKJV);

And He said to them, "Take heed and beware of covetousness, for one's life does not consist in the abundance of the things he possesses." Then He spoke a parable to them, saying: "The ground of a certain rich man yielded plentifully. And he thought within himself, saying, 'What shall I do, since I have no room to store my crops?' So he said, 'I will do this: I will pull down my barns and build greater, and there I will store all my crops and my goods. And I will say to my soul, "Soul, you have many goods laid up for many years; take your ease; eat, drink, and be merry." ' But God said to him, 'Fool! This night your soul will be required of you; then whose will those things be which you have provided?' "So is he who lays up treasure for himself, and is not rich toward God."

God doesn't want us to lay up treasure for ourselves. Why? Because what He gives us belongs to Him and is for the kingdom. The rich man in the story didn't understand stewardship, neither did he care about God's kingdom. Friend, you must give your things to God; otherwise, you will mistake them for your own and forget who gave them to you. We are just stewarding of His blessings.

I recently got a revelation of what that really means at my new church home. When I say God will work this thing out called life for our good, I mean that from personal experiences. The point I am in my life, I have been able to look at current situations and connect the dots back to past situations. I do this for several reasons:

1. To RISE in amazement of where God has brought me from.

2. To REVIVE my faith and trust in knowing God works all things together for my good.

3. To RELEASE that feeling of defeat that fear gave in that past situation, making room for the victory that God gave me in my current situation and for the future.

This allowed me to connect two-plus years to now. It midway began when my husband and I lost a relationship with friends that led us to part ways for a while. Of course, we were hurt at first! After a while, I know God was revealing to me that we are being set apart for something.

Most times, you are not being set apart to be alone but to allow a new strand of influence to summon you to another environment. As a result of that separation, we met someone that we wouldn't have crossed paths with if we continued the old path. That person invited us to our current church home.

Within our first three visits, I had chosen to read a book that the congregation was about to begin reading and studying. This book changed and elevated my mindset on giving, tithes, and offerings. It was written by Robert Morris called *The Blessed Life*. My Pastor played out one of the principles. He stated that he needed $150 cash from somebody. A Deacon sitting in the front of the church got up so fast. I was lost as to how did he put that money up there so fast without even counting what's in his pockets or anything? Wondering, did he get a word from God prior to service and already had it? Did he plan on using it for something else but felt that was more important? But I guess all that matters is that somebody had what he needed.

The Pastor explained that he had given the $150 to the Deacon prior to the start of service and only instructed him to give him the money when he asked for it quickly. That's all the Deacon knew. This demonstration modeled the spirit we as His people should have when it comes to God, tithe, and giving. We have to come to the realization that the tithe (10% of your increase) is not ours to keep in the first place. The tithe is God's that we are to give to His kingdom, which is stewardship. We are stewards of the things He gives us. That's why we tithe, get married before Him and christen our children. Our most valuable things are what we should return and declare as His.

When we think these things are "ours," we attach to it or love it on another level, forcing it sometimes to be put before God. It is only right to love our spouse and children, but not more than God. Isn't this an incredible way to live? It eliminates unhealthy competition and comparison, strife, covetousness, envy, etc.

2 Corinthians 9:10 reveals a great mystery; *"Now may He who supplies seed to the sower, and bread for food, supply and multiply the seed you have sown and increase the fruits of your righteousness."* The farmer's seed belongs to God, and so does the bread your family eats. He takes responsibility for them. Therefore, if he gives it, there should be no trouble giving it back to Him.

Surely, if God trusts you as a faithful steward, He will always provide for you. You see, developing a stewardship mindset gives you an assurance that God will always supply your needs. All you need to do is ensure that you're a steward God can trust.

The Ultimate source

The spirit of mammon develops a love for money within us that opens the door of selfishness, greed, jealousy, envy, and discrediting of God. We must not forget that God is "The Ultimate Source" that supplies everything we need, such as resources.

In the Old Testament, God made manna to fall from heaven. However, He doesn't use the same strategy today. God uses channels to provide for us. These channels are physical structures or even people that provide help or sustenance. But the Bible teaches us that God is the behind-the-scenes-provider.

John 3:27 says, *"...A man can receive nothing, except it be given him from heaven."* These words were spoken by John the Baptist concerning his ministry. When Jesus became famous, some Jews attempted to pitch John against Jesus. They told him that the man he baptized was becoming more famous. Certainly, any other person would have listened to them and despised Jesus.

However, John knew better; he understood something they didn't- God is the ultimate source. Whether it's money, fame, or influence, it comes from God. Yes, it can come through associates or jobs, but it's from God. Do you see where many of our troubles come from? We see channels as sources. The truth is, your source is constant, but your channels aren't constant. So stop worrying whenever people decide to cut you off.

Has a beneficiary or sponsor stopped supporting you? Well, don't fret. God is the ultimate source. Are you upset with a friend or loved one because they wouldn't help you? Understand that God hasn't chosen them as His channels for your blessings. This mindset will heal your relationships and take the pressure off. Stop worrying about who will help you or what job can sustain your family. Rather, focus on God – the ultimate source.

Do you have so many needs? Maybe you're in debt or in the middle of a crisis. Look at what Philippians 4:19 says, *"But my God shall supply all your need according to his riches in glory by Christ Jesus."* Friend, is He your God? Then He'll supply all your needs. And yes, "all" is in that text just in case you think God is only concerned about the big or "spiritual" things. Your whole life is God's business, and when He supplies, He takes care of all your needs.

Here are some reasons we should remember God as our Ultimate source?

1. To trust and depend on Him alone.

2. To ensure that our trust isn't in ourselves.

3. To ensure that our trust isn't in people

4. To have the peace to give

5. To become faithful stewards of God's resources

6. To enable us to seek God's kingdom and not material things

7. To give us hope when we lose material possessions

8. To have faith in God's limitless supply

In Deuteronomy 8:18, Moses admonished the Israelites to remember that God was the source of their power to get wealth. He wanted them always to remember God when they took in abundance around them.

For instance, a wealthy Jew named Joseph wakes up in the money and sees his cattle grazing in the open fields. They are thousands of them, and difficult to count some days. What comes to Joseph's heart at that moment is that God is behind his prosperity. It came from God, God will sustain it, and so it can be controlled by God. Moses reminded the Israelites who their source was because they could forget. Do you know what happens when we forget that God is our source? We begin to worship and honor channels. In fact, we tend to serve money which God created to serve us when we forget who our source is.

So, whenever you're worried about bills or giving becomes difficult, remember your source. James 1:17 *describes God as our ultimate source in a profound way. It says, "Every good gift and every perfect gift is from above, and cometh down from the Father of lights, with whom is no variableness, neither shadow of turning."* What you seek is from God, so look to God and nowhere else. If you focus on Him, your life will be good, perfect, and without sorrow.

Finally, examine your heart today and identify what's in charge. Is it a desire for God's will or a desire for material things? The true test of your worship is what your heart esteems the most; make sure your heart esteems God, He is love!

Chapter 3:

GOD IS my joy

(You shall not take the name of the Lord your God in vain)

My Sweetness,

I just woke up from a dream about a woman I saw walking along the beach. Let me tell you because I just talked to *Impatience* about it. Her walk was so graceful. She's the one who turned beauty into beautiful. Her skin was sun-kissed, smooth as honey, and sweet as brown sugar. The wind blew just enough to blow her hair off her back. She wore her hair long with a slight curl in it, like a Finesse commercial. The woman had a demeanor about her that spoke boldness but a smile that sang psalms. You could see that her confidence was impeccable, but she was not arrogant at all.

What made her stand out to me was the glow she had. Her glow was warm, inviting, and like a layer of protection amongst a small crowd of people. I couldn't explain anything outside of that, but it was just something about her. I could only imagine if God were to bless me with a woman of such ambiance. But it left me wanting to get a closer look at her.

As I walked softly behind her, the sound of my feet sinking into the white sand was masked by the crashing of the waves. I noticed that she was not walking in a straight line but veering off to the right toward the ocean. She continued to walk in that same direction, but as she got closer to the water, the waves were calming down. Suddenly, she stopped, turned around, and seeing me, she began to walk towards me, but away from the water. That's when two things became known, the waves of the ocean began crashing again and that the woman was you.

It was like the ocean knew you were near, but the further away you got, it got upset. Did the ocean want your presence? Was it lonely? I wasn't sure what was going on; all I knew was that you were heading towards me. You were about ten feet away from me when you stopped, smiled at me, and walked back toward the water to vanish. I recognized that the physical aspect of our roles in the dream was reversed.

The woman represented the trust you have in me, and the ocean was you. When you are in a situation where things feel like they're crashing down on you, I come to calm you. God stands there and watches you, as you handle things. I felt as though she would have come closer in the dream if it were not for the ocean feeling forgotten…

Have You Been There Before?

How do you respond when life refuses to give you the things you desire most? Or when it seems God has turned His back on you? Not everyone is as strong as Job, or as meek as Jesus. Job worshipped God amid great crisis. In Jesus's case, He called out to the God who forsook Him on the cross. These are instances where holy men experienced the true absence of God's presence. In the end, it turned out for good. In comparison, what we experience as God's absence is our ignorance or insensitivity.

Most times, we feel God is far away; He's closer than we can imagine. Think about it. Can a faithful God forsake you when you need Him the most? Even when He has promised to be your ever-present help in times of need. It's this unbelief that makes us give in to fear. But it doesn't end at fear. We begin to doubt other attributes of God, like His forgiveness and mercy. As a result, we open our arms wide to frustration and anger.

Frustration comes because instead of trusting in God's report, we believe more in our limitations. On the other hand, anger permits our heart when we think God is against us and never truly forgave us. These are feelings I experienced in a season of delay. What I wanted the most eluded me. During this period, my enemy took advantage of my circumstance. I was convinced that God wasn't with me. In fact, I believed that He was responsible for my pain and enjoyed seeing me afflicted.

However, the Bible paints a picture of a merciful God who is moved by the cries of His people. He searches our hearts and satisfies our desires. When God's people were in captivity for four hundred and thirty years, they cried out to God and sent them help.

In another circumstance, Isaac's wife, Rebekah, was barren, so he called on God. Not long after, Rebekah became pregnant. There are many testimonies in the scriptures of ordinary people who had extraordinary faith in God. They called out to Him in their stormy seasons, and He rescued them.

Now, if God is so faithful and near us, why do we give in to frustration and anger the moment we encounter hardship. Is it because we don't understand that breakthroughs only come after great suffering? Perhaps we forget that God works all things together for our good? Or maybe we just don't know how to respond in faith, even in the darkest times.

Have you been neck-deep in frustration and anger? Have you gotten to your wit's end? Did anything happen to make you want to give up? Maybe you finally decided to accept your fate, whatever it was. Well, I've been there. But I'm so glad that I scaled through. Yes, I faced challenges that made me dishonor God in my heart by doubting His character. I want to share with you the story of my frustration and anger. Certainly, it'll help you understand how clueless we can be. Often, we forget that God's hand doesn't have to be visible in our lives to believe that He's at work. God sure does love to reveal Himself. But much more, He loves working behind the scenes.

Job's experience reveals a lot about the suffering of a believer. But it also shows us that God works behind the scenes. Job 23:8-10 says, *"Look, I go forward, but He is not there, And backward, but I cannot perceive Him; When He works on the left hand, I cannot behold Him; When He turns to the right hand, I cannot see Him. But He knows the way that I take; When He has tested me, I shall come forth as gold."* From this text, you see that God is at work even in Job's seemingly hopeless situation. I also had a seemingly hopeless situation, but I didn't know that God was working on the object of my pain.

Truth is frustration and anger thrive on our ignorance. Job's actions during his trial seasons were strange. Why? Because they were the actions of a man who knew how God works. No wonder he could worship God and remain faithful when his whole world came crashing down. In the verses above, Job refers to his suffering as a test. He said, *"When he hath tried me, I shall come forth as gold."* What a profound statement. He was in the furnace of affliction, yet he could see better days ahead.

Indeed, the days after God restored Job was his golden days. But how did he pull through without cursing God? How did he conquer the anger and frustration that threatened to explode within him? He knew that there was gain in pain. Yes, Job understood that when a blessing seems delayed, it's because God is planning something beautiful.

One thing I learned from the experience I'm about to share with you is that frustration and anger with God can nip your miracle in the bud. It can steal your testimony and limit God's hand from reaching you.

Let's Have a Baby

My husband and I had been tossing back and forth the idea of us having one more child together. At that time, he had a thirteen-year-old daughter from a previous marriage. I also had a 10-

year-old daughter from a previous relationship. In a way, we are a blended family.

A blended family happens when two single parents with children come together to make a family. I guess it's "blended" because the parents and their kids are already families. Most times, blended families are formed by divorcees. But in my case, I wasn't married before I met Abraham, so it's different. Because we weren't a couple without kids, having children wasn't at the top of our priority list when we got married.

However, we had two options. We could allow our daughters to grow up together and wonder how life would be adding one more to the family tying all of us together. Speaking for myself, I had already had a child out of wedlock and wouldn't mind doing it the right way with the love of my life. A child, a life with a mixture of my husband and me, was what I imagined for our lives. Not to mention, he had already displayed that he was a great father figure for my daughter and a great father to his daughter.

Abe understood what this meant for me, to partially heal and redeem myself from my past of becoming a teen mother in my mind. Even though I was no longer the teenage girl who got pregnant out of wedlock, the shadow of my mistake still loomed over my life. Although I should have known that I couldn't redeem myself, I wanted the peace of having a child the right way. A part of me seemed to believe that my happiness wouldn't be complete without this child. Indeed, if I didn't have a way to shield myself from the embarrassment of my past, it would always hunt me.

Eventually, Abe came around to the decision to add to our tribe. I had not realized that I had been battling this still. Why can't I get past this? Is it because I fear that I missed out on experiencing life and fully getting to know myself? Am I still not satisfied or whole with myself and where I am? Could I have been further in life and have more going for myself and my family? Or am I just afraid that I am not enough for my husband because I am not confident enough within myself? I struggled with these feelings whenever I thought about having another child. This is a typical case of the past interfering with the future. I know I'm not alone in this area.

What past mistakes have you refused to let go of? What do you keep beating yourself up about? Is your present life a mere attempt to undo what you did in the past? Well, taking on such a huge challenge is not your job.

The last time I checked, God is our redeemer; we have no power to redeem ourselves. But during the time I fought within myself,

I didn't let God play his part and heal my heart. It was a season of inner struggle and turbulent thoughts.

However, if you were on the outside looking in, you would never know this. I promised myself that no matter what, I would not let them see me sweat! Although this mindset made me strong, it alienated me from people God would have used to help me. The whole world wasn't against me or waiting for my failure as I thought. Instead, the enemy was within, the fear I kept nurturing and listening to.

On the upside, I am married to who God ordained me to be with; we have a home, each have a car, some savings, two incomes coming in the household, and he wants to now try at having a baby. This was a different feeling, a good feeling. I always wanted to know what it meant to intentionally have a baby, and it is okay with life, no judgment, just excitement.

For me, this meant showing my daughter how she should want life to go for her. If I would have had my oldest at 30 years old, just imagine the time I would have been allowed to be more experienced with life. Yes, I know you can never be fully prepared for being a parent but being aware of yourself helps you be a better person for the next.

It's different when it's a choice that's not frowned upon and being obedient to God's way. My mistake didn't make life easy for me. Being forced to grow up while hearing the whispers, seeing the backstabbing, and knowing you disobeyed God can be a heavy load that some can't bear to carry. Imagine a little girl who had hopes and dreams, now obligated to set them aside and nurture a baby that wasn't in the scope of things. Those years it seemed like there was no light at the end of the tunnel. At least, I can say I did make it this far!

Does God Hold a Grudge?

We tried for one month, two months, three months, and nothing happened, so we had figured we might need to have a physical done. At least myself, I was knocking at thirty years old at that time. Not to mention, I had been on the Depo Provera shot for ten years from when my daughter was born until after I got married. Glad to say everything came back fine, but the doctor did say that being on that type of birth control for that long period of time could prolong the "trying" stage if I could even get pregnant at all. I left that doctor's appointment feeling guilty, frustrated, and once again, I "messed up."

Gradually, I began to question God's complete forgiveness. I call myself preventing any further mishaps, not realizing that it's not the birth control. It was the fact that there were possibilities that I could have been pregnant if it were not for the shot. I must

73

be honest; I was still having sex. That is the act that is required to get pregnant again. DUH! So Ebony, were you afraid of it happening again? Or were you so upset that it happened or that God allowed it to happen? Did you just choose to take matters into your own hands?

Apparently, I had more trust in the shot than in God getting me through this and following His way until we got married. This is where the fear, the anger, the blame, the hurt, and the regret turned me cold. Now that my mind was made up to have another baby and my husband is on board, I fear that we may not be able to have a child after all. I am angry that everyone else can have a baby, multiple babies, and not planned. How could this happen like this? God, can't you pull off one of your miracles for a family who wants a baby? Are you still punishing me?

These questions occupied my heart. My mind kept going back to the mistake I made in the past. I felt God didn't want me to have more children because of my sin. The fact that I still felt ashamed and guilty about my past made me consider my sin as unforgivable. And in my fear, I believed that God thought the same thing. It felt like God held a grudge against me and would make sure I went through hell. Imagine how miserable life would be if you did something that God could never forgive you of. Certainly, you'll live in fear and torment, always looking over your shoulder. I was in such a position, and it produced anger and frustration. In the long run, it hardened my heart a bit.

You might be in such a situation right now. Well, you don't need to go too far in your journey to realize the truth. If I had snapped out of my guilt and shame early enough to remember that God could never hold a grudge, life would have been easier. You see, so many times we try to fight alone when we're in trouble. We live God standing on the sidelines and blame Him for doing nothing. But the question is, did we invite Him to help? Did we turn the battle over to Him? Or did we start making assumptions about the reason for our suffering?

What are you going through right now? Do you think it's because of your awful past? Are you convinced God holds a grudge and is out to get you? In truth, you can never understand God's forgiving nature until you look at scriptures that reveal His character. For instance, Psalm 103:8 -10 says, *"The LORD is merciful and gracious, slow to anger, and plenteous in mercy. He will not always chide: neither will he keep his anger for ever. He hath not dealt with us after our sins; nor rewarded us according to our iniquities."* There are three things to note in these verses:

1. God is merciful and gracious – He pardons sin. No matter what you've done, God can choose to overlook

them and rescue you from the consequences of your actions.

2. God is slow to anger – He's not taking account of every sin you've committed. God is patient with those He loves and gives room for repentance.

3. God doesn't deal with us according to our sins – No matter what you do, God won't treat you like a low-lie or a wretch. He won't think the worst of you. Neither will He punish you according to the weight of your sin.

This last point may be hard to understand, but it happened with Cain. Cain committed the first murder in the Bible. He killed his brother, Abel, out of jealousy, and God punished him for it. However, Cain told God that he couldn't bear the punishment, and God made it more bearable. Genesis 4:13-15 (KJV)says *"And Cain said unto the LORD, My punishment is greater than I can bear. Behold, thou hast driven me out this day from the face of the earth; and from thy face shall I be hid; and I shall be a fugitive and a vagabond in the earth; and it shall come to pass, that every one that findeth me shall slay me. **And the LORD said unto him, Therefore whosoever slayeth Cain, vengeance shall be taken on him sevenfold. And the LORD set a mark upon Cain, lest any finding him should kill him.**"*

Also, there's concrete proof in scriptures that when you confess your mistakes to God, He doesn't remember them. Instead, He gives you a new life and restores everything you've lost. Isaiah 43:18-21 (KJV) says, *"Remember ye not the former things, neither consider the things of old. Behold, I will do a new thing; now it shall spring forth; shall ye not know it? I will even make a way in the wilderness, and rivers in the desert. The beast of the field shall honour me, the dragons and the owls: because I give waters in the wilderness, and rivers in the desert, to give drink to my people, my chosen. This people have I formed for myself; they shall shew forth my praise."*

Pay attention to God's words in Isaiah 43:25-26: *"I, even I, am he that blotteth out thy transgressions for mine own sake, and will not remember thy sins. Put me in remembrance: let us plead together: declare thou, that thou mayest be justified."* Do you understand the implication of God's words? Although you might remember your mistakes and think they still have power over you, God has removed them from existence. His word reveals that He forgets about your past. Surely, God won't make you pay for a sin He has forgotten. In fact, the scripture above reveals that God treats your past like it never happened. Therefore, you ought to stop worrying about something that never happened, even though you believe you have physical evidence. For example, my daughter is the evidence that I got pregnant out of wedlock, yet it doesn't make God's forgiveness any less real.

Also, I blamed myself for not being fully responsible for abstaining from sex, so that pregnancy was not an option. I was also blaming God for allowing my past to affect this part of my life too. This is a whole new chapter! I'm hurt just because I didn't want another kid at first, and now, when I do, I may not be able to.

Regret only settled in when I realized the decisions I made for the present were now affecting my future. This cycle has to end with me; it has to! We chose just to keep moving forward with trying. I'm so glad my husband is not a quitter; he keeps me going. That's how I know we're meant to be each of our strengths compliments the other's weaknesses.

The truth about my fear of retribution was that I didn't understand God's love enough. Because of the difficulty in taking in, I couldn't see past my wrong. You know, God's forgiveness brings freedom from condemnation. Nevertheless, since I didn't understand that I had been forgiven, I felt condemned. Do you remember the scene in the Bible about Jesus and a Jewish woman who was caught in adultery? According to the Law of Moses, she should be sentenced to death by stoning. But in the nick of time, Jesus swooped in and saved her. How did He do it? He merely showed her accusers that they were also sinners and not in the position to judge justice.

As a result, every man who had lifted a stone against this woman dropped his stone and went home. Jesus's final words to the adulterous woman were, "neither do I condemn you, go and sin no more." This story shows that no matter how I felt about my past, God didn't condemn me. In the same way, God doesn't condemn you. Instead, Rom 8:33-34 (KJV) says, *"Who shall lay any thing to the charge of God's elect? It is God that justifieth. Who is he that condemneth? It is Christ that died, yea rather, that is risen again, who is even at the right hand of God, who also maketh intercession for us."* Did you notice in this text that God is your justifier? So whenever you experience difficulties and you feel condemned, it's not from God.

Giving God an Ultimatum

We continued to try for six more months. During that, I became bitter and prepared myself if we can't have any more kids. I also declared that if I wasn't pregnant by my 30th birthday, it was a done deal for that possibility. We'd get a dog or something if it comes down to that. This was an ultimatum. I was fed up with trying because I believed that the time to have a baby was slipping by. But the truth is, no matter how frustrated and angry you get, you can't hurry God.

 In the Bible, Sarah tried to hasten God's plans but ended up creating more pain for her family. As humans, we can get emotional when things don't go our way. We set unrealistic standards for ourselves and deadlines that aren't in line with God's plan for our lives. Consider Sarah and Abraham, who felt they couldn't have their own child. They understood that according to natural laws, they had passed the age for procreation. In their case, they had a real limitation; their bodies were old and frail. Yet, God isn't restricted by natural laws, stereotypes, and deadlines.

Take a look at **Ecclesiastes 3:1-8**, *"To every thing, there is a season, and a time to every purpose under the heaven: A time to be born, and a time to die; a time to plant, and a time to pluck up that which is planted; A time to kill, and a time to heal; a time to break down, and a time to build up; A time to weep, and a time to laugh; a time to mourn, and a time to dance; A time to cast away stones, and a time to gather stones together; a time to embrace, and a time to refrain from embracing; A time to get, and a time to lose; a time to keep, and a time to cast away; A time to rend, and a time to sew; a time to keep silence, and a time to speak; A time to love, and a time to hate; a time of war,* *and a time of peace. "These verses show the various things that have allotted time in this life.*

However, Ecclesiastes 3:11 (KJV) says, *"He hath made everything beautiful in his time…"* So, there's a natural time for everything but also a supernatural time – God's own time. And the difference between these two is that everything is picture-perfect in God's time. There's no error or room for regrets. For instance, I was so ashamed of my past because I had gotten pregnant at the wrong time. But I knew that having a baby in marriage was good and would bring beauty, yet my approach was wrong.

Giving God an ultimatum never works because it won't last if you receive anything outside His time. At that point in my life, what I needed was patience. But how could I be patent without faith? Fear had taken the place of my faith. It has replaced peace and patience with frustration and anger. I was so agitated because I couldn't bear the thought of never having a child with Abe.

I know I'm not the only one who has given God an ultimatum. Some people have even threatened to stop believing if they don't get their requests. Funnily enough, sometimes God allows us to go ahead and stop believing. We can't change God, but we can move His hand through faith and patience. That's how we obtain

God's promises. But impatience and anger blind us to God's help in seasons of trial.

I had some hard moments at work during this time as well. In my position, I had the pleasure of registering applications for any type of public assistance. Due to the issue at hand, I would hate receiving applications for women having several kids, been on public assistance for several years, and stating that the father was not in the household. Questioning God, why is it that she can continue to have kids, but I can't? Why does one seem to be better than the other or more deserving than the other with you? I would literally need to take a break with my husband so that I could vent and cry to him to make it through the day.

There was a time I could remember when I sent him an email venting, and he sent me back a powerful prayer that I did have enough sense to keep for when I did have the mind to pray. I mean, I wasn't trying to judge their situations, but I was scared, hurt, and angry. I was so cold and belittling God, as though He does not know what He is doing.

Three months later, my birthday came. It was my 30th, and I hadn't planned a trip, gathering, or anything. I was now depressed. I went on playing it off with my family as though I had been too busy, and it had slipped my mind. So my husband declared we're doing something for our anniversary, which was slightly over a month later. We had planned a weekend getaway.

About three weeks later, I had realized I had missed my period, thinking it was stress. I told Abe, and the first thing out of his mouth was, "Did you take a pregnancy test?" So, I went to the store, purchased one, and took it the following morning. When I say in God's timing, I mean it! WE WERE PREGNANT! Did God hear my husband's prayers? He must have felt sorry for us, lol. I was so overwhelmed with excitement and disbelief while I took another test right before the getaway. We enjoyed ourselves.

Doubt dishonors God

When we returned, I had my first doc appt. We got our due date, and I knew exactly the moment she was conceived. I returned to work the next day, and something dawned on me. That moment I had emailed my husband angrily and he sent me back the prayer. I searched through my emails, not knowing exactly what I was looking for, but I just wanted to read it again. There it is! I reread his prayer first because I knew my response after he needed some prayer, LOL.

After I finished reading it all, I was about to back out of it. Until I scrolled back up and looked at the date this email was sent. Surprisingly as at that time I was already pregnant! God had already made his delivery, but I was too busy being angry from fear. That anger did not bring honor to God; it brought me doubt about Him. When you doubt God, you are downplaying Him, His name, and His word. So, stay in faith, and know where your joy comes from!

Chapter 4:

GOD IS my peace

(Remember the Sabbath day, to keep it holy)

My girl,

I am so proud of how strong-willed you have been lately. I have to acknowledge the hard work you have been putting in. You are making your way, being fit for your crown. You have a life to lead for your daughter. Taking every opportunity to make way for you and ensuring that your family is a top priority.

Ungrateful told me that you were holding back from opportunities that would help provide for your family. Do you think God would be opposed to you taking care of you and your daughter? If He would be, what does that say about His integrity and priorities? You are supposedly His child, and He wouldn't like anything to hold Him back from you. You are blooming into the growing flower that you are, so continue to water your life with the zeal to get what you want and need. He should be willing to help you every step of the way.

You will only continue to shine if you grind. Don't be afraid to rock the boat; you have to be willing to paddle to get somewhere. You are my fresh air of inspiration. You give me confidence every day, and I thank you for that. You are the water that flows through the river of my soul. You are the sun in my sky. You are the breath that fills my body with life. The life that you are setting yourself up for is putting you on the path to success. You are the source for all the good things in me. There is unimaginable joy and happiness in me because of you. I want you to continue to strive to be better. Don't let anyone or anything get in your way.

Where does your strength come from? It comes from within you. You are your greatest source. You have gotten promotions on your terms, finding your way to what fits you, and being confident in it. I also know that your God is a jealous god. He is not happy when you find

another way to your goals. It is hurtful to know that He can be that way instead of making

things work. But as I always say, I will always have your back, even when you don't have your own.

Love, Fear

Time Set Apart

Around the world, there are many arguments about what day of the week is the Sabbath. Some bible scholars believe that Saturday and not Sunday is the Sabbath. But most people believe that the Sabbath day is Sunday. So, this chapter isn't about proving which day of the week is the Lord's Day. Sunday is accepted by most Christians as the Sabbath and the day Jesus rose from the dead. The Sabbath day is as old as the world. When God created the heavens and the earth, He worked for six days and rested on the seventh. Because of this, He sanctified the seventh day and required His people to keep it holy.

The Sabbath should be set apart from any other day of the week because God has ordained it as a day of rest. Through this pattern, it's clear that God approves of a six-day work schedule. Working five days a week isn't wrong, but the scriptures show us that working six days a week isn't wrong either.

Look at what the Bible says about the Sabbath day in Exodus 20:8-11: *"8 Remember the Sabbath day, to keep it holy. Six days you shall labor and do all your work, but the seventh day is the Sabbath of the Lord your God. In it you shall do no work: you, nor your son, nor your daughter, nor your male servant, nor your female servant, nor your cattle, nor your stranger who is within your gates. For in six days the Lord made the heavens and the earth, the sea, and all that is in them, and rested the seventh day. Therefore the Lord blessed the Sabbath day and hallowed it."*

Do you see that God's plan for you is a six-day work schedule at the most? He desires that you work hard as a believer. But God doesn't want your work to take over your life. Think about it; if God, who is all-powerful, had a day to rest from His work, then you should have a day of complete rest. Does it surprise you that God cares about your physical and mental health? God is concerned about every aspect of your life and doesn't want any to suffer.

In the 21st Century, people have become obsessed with their work and tend to work round-the-clock, every day of the week, including the Sabbath. It has become more difficult to rest because some people never take a day off. This isn't God's will for the believer. It's possible to take a day off every week and still be tremendously successful. Don't join the unbelieving crowd to chance material things and money.

Most times, people find it difficult to rest because their heart isn't dependent on God. They set out to make all the money they can by their strength. Since people get paid according to the time they put in, it's difficult to set aside time for yourself and God.

In truth, if you don't see God as your source and depend on Him to bless you, you can lose yourself in the pursuit of success.

Ask yourself this question; do you have the ability to provide for all your needs? How much money can you generate from your work for your family? There's a reason God is the supplier of all our needs. Also, there's a reason Jesus asks us to stop worrying about material things. If we don't subscribe to God's resting program and trust Him to provide for all our needs, materialism will consume our hearts.

Much more than physical rest, the Sabbath day signifies our dependence on God. Why? Because when you identify God as your Lord and sustainer, you will obey His word and live according to His standards. Ezekiel 20:11-12 says, *11 And I gave them My statutes and showed them My judgments, 'which, if a man does, he shall live by them.' 12 Moreover I also gave them My Sabbaths, to be a sign between them and Me, that they might know that I am the Lord who sanctifies them. "*

You see, keeping the Sabbath is a sign that you belong to God. God wants you to observe the Sabbath; remember that He's the Lord that sanctifies you. What does it mean to be sanctified? It means to be separated, set apart, or purified for a particular purpose. God desires to make a difference between you and those who don't serve Him. Sundays might be ordinary to

89

everyone else, but God wants you to regard it as a holy day. So, you can't work on Sundays like you work every other day.

God Gives Us Work

What's your attitude towards work? Do you know where work comes from? Do you know what it means? Most people get obsessed or worried about work because they don't know who gives work. Genesis 2:15 says, *"15 Then the Lord God took the man and put him in the garden of Eden to tend and keep it."*

In this text, the Bible reveals that God put Adam in the Garden of Eden to work. God was the first person with a job because He rested from His work. Also, He was the first employer because He hired Adam as the keeper of the Garden. When it comes to work, most people believe God has nothing to do with it. They regard work to be a secular activity. However, work has its origin in God. It can be used to fulfill His purposes. Work is worth it!

God made man to fulfill His purpose, and Adam was going to do that through his work. Therefore, work isn't all about earning a living. To God, work is manifesting the potential God has deposited within you. It is manifesting you to benefit God, His kingdom, and humanity. True work is the expression of purpose and destiny. Ultimately, it's completely spiritual.

God didn't establish the Sabbath day because He's against work; think about it. Yes, He set aside one day for rest, but He ordained six days for work. Do you see how vital work is? God isn't saying, "I hate the fact that you work, sit around and do nothing on Sunday." No, God is saying, "your work is important, so I've given you six days to pursue purpose and success. But I want you to rest just as I rested on the seventh day. Rest so that I can work on your behalf. Rest and understand that it's not just about your effort or ability."

When you choose to rise to the demands of God, your work receives God's supernatural influence and blessing when you rest. God comes down to revive your strength and passion. He will release new ideas into your mind. Your father comes in times of refreshing from heaven and takes over your battles. As you RISE, REVIVE, and RELEASE, He is working things out.

Psalm 46:10-11 (NKJV) says, *"10 Be still, and know that I am God; I will be exalted among the nations, I will be exalted in the earth! 11 The Lord of hosts is with us; The God of Jacob is our refuge. Selah"* When you live by your efforts, you're living below God's will for you. He wants you to live a life of fullness and abundance. Not just material abundance, but physical and

91

spiritual abundance. God wants your life to be filled with peace no man can fathom. However, only those who yield to God's command to be still will ever experience such peace.

Imagine life without anxiety and self-dependence. You'll agree with me that many of life's problems come from trying to do things without God. But God teaches us in His word how to depend on Him. The Sabbath day signifies the typical state of heart of a believer – rest.

Your work is from God, so it shouldn't take you away from God. The Bible says that God is before all things. Don't think God doesn't care whether you can provide three square meals for your family. He's the creator of work. In fact, God's word teaches us the attitude to have towards work. Let's just look at three scriptures that show what a believer should do about their work.

1. **Work diligently** - Ecclesiastes 9:10 (NKJV) says, *"10 Whatever your hand finds to do, do it with your might; for there is no work or device or knowledge or wisdom in the grave where you are going."* You see, work only exists in this physical world. So God expects you to be dedicated and committed to whatever He's given you.

2. **Commit your work to God** - Proverbs 16:3 (NKJV) says, *"3 Commit your works to the Lord, And your*

thoughts will be established." Your work shouldn't make you independent of God. Instead, you should depend on God to bless your work. Therefore, it should be your daily practice to commit your job or career to God.

3. **Work like God owns the company** - Colossians 3:23 (NKJV) says, *"23 And whatever you do, do it heartily, as to the Lord and not to men, ... "* Is God asking you to pretend? Is He saying you should just act like He's the owner of that job? No! This scripture reveals that whatever you do as a believer should be seen as a service to God. The earth is His and its fullness, and so is that job or career.

These scriptures clearly show that God isn't against work. Therefore, the Sabbath isn't going to affect your work or make you lose money. The Sabbath day is a blessing to man. Look at it as paid time off; you will reap the benefits of being obedient to His commandments.

The Sabbath is for you

While Jesus was on the earth, the Pharisees and Sadducees disagreed with Him on keeping the Sabbath holy. Without knowing it, they had a wrong perspective of the Sabbath. They thought that they were slaves of the Sabbath. To them, it was just a religious holiday to be observed. They didn't keep the Sabbath holy because they understood it but as an obligation. It means that a Jew in that era might be with God on Sunday because he or she couldn't carry out their normal work activities. They kept it grudgingly and made sure everyone else suffered "the punishment of the Sabbath."

Such a disagreement occurred in Mark 2:23-28. Look at what transpired: *"23 Now it happened that He went through the grainfields on the Sabbath; and as they went His disciples began to pluck the heads of grain. 24 And the Pharisees said to Him, "Look, why do they do what is not lawful on the Sabbath?" But He said to them, "Have you never read what David did when he was in need and hungry, he and those with him how he went into the house of God in the days of Abiathar the high priest, and ate the showbread, which is not lawful to eat, except for the priests, and also gave some to those who were with him?" And He said to them, "The Sabbath was made for man, and not man for the Sabbath. Therefore the Son of Man is also Lord of the Sabbath."*

Jesus taught them to have a different perspective. The Sabbath wasn't made as a law to burden man. Rather, the Sabbath is a blessing and a gift. Yes, the Sabbath day was made for you. It's an expression of God's loving-kindness towards His people.

Your rest and maintaining peace are important with all the things that are coming against you to deter you from your purpose. A wise man once said that "life is a battlefield." It's full of challenges and oppositions. You must fight to be successful. Well, amid the struggle, you need to recharge and refuel for the next battle. Always working is sure to lead to burnout or a breakdown. The absence of rest leads to stress and anxiety, which is opposed to relaxation and peace. If you want a more peaceful and fulfilling life, then you can't downplay the importance of rest.

The Perfect Job!

I can share so much about observing the Sabbath and not working on Sundays because I've been there. I allowed so much to override what God asked me to do, even when it was beneficial for me. I started working at a hospital as a dishwasher and kitchen help. When I was initially hired, I specifically stated that I don't work on Sundays. Now, I'm sure you know where I'm going with this. I had good Christian principles, and I believed in the Sabbath. But I never knew that a job would interfere with what I already knew.

Right before I applied for that job, I had just rededicated my life back to God. I figured He blessed me with a higher-paying job right after, so the least I could do is try to honor His commandments. I vividly remember it was the third job of my work history.

I got this job by God's grace. At the time, it belonged to another person, and I was only filling in for her. A lady went off on medical leave that worked in the kitchen's office as an operator who took the food orders for the patients. Then, I had worked in fast food, retail, and now in the hospital. I have a good work ethic and a versatile work history. I was trying to find out what I liked to do or what field I wanted to work, in the long run. I did not like staying on my feet the entire time of my shift, so I wanted to experience an office setting. Even though I was healthy and could stand for long hours if necessary, I desired a desk job.

I got acquainted with the kitchen managers and expressed my interest in filling in for the lady that had to be off work temporarily. They immediately went for it and moved me to the office. Now, this is the grace of God at work. Certainly, I didn't expect them to refuse, but then it felt too easy.

As soon as I sat down in front of the computer, I sighed like, "This is the feeling I want." That was a give-away that I needed a sit-down job. I can still get up on breaks, go to the printer, or customize an order in the kitchen. It was not a job you would quickly get a flat butt from. There was movement, which I still liked.

The next thing I found out is that I'm good at speaking to people by phone. My number of completed calls quickly came up to the workers who had been in there. This was for me! I figured I need to make an impression so that they see I'm more effective in here than out there. Sincerely, I just wanted to be diligent enough to be trusted with that position for the long haul.

In retrospect, I should have put my trust in God for job security rather than trying to please people. Still, it's good to show your employers that employing you wasn't a bad decision. I was hoping to get at least three to six months of experience there to have decent working experience in that field to apply for another office position when she returned. That's exactly what I did. They kept me in there because she could not return; she retired. I wasn't sure if she was sick or not, hoping she was okay but still grateful for the promotion. Oh, did I mention that I was over $1 raise going to that position? God did it again in less than six months. I enjoyed what I was doing!

A Subtle Temptation

I was having a swell time at my job. But I never knew that something would make me compromise. You know, it's so easy to be resolute when you don't have what you're asking God for. Before I got the job, I made up my mind not to work on Sundays. I decided to keep to my spiritual commitment and stay devoted to God. I didn't want material things to get a hold of my heart. So yes, I wanted God to be at the center of my heart. You can say I was on guard because I even mentioned it to my employers. However, sin or compromise doesn't come in like a flood. Temptation is always subtle.

Do you remember how Eve got deceived by the devil in the Garden of Eden? He was subtle; he indirectly attacked her faith in God and got her to commit treason. Well, the same thing happened in my life concerning work. I was working so hard and impressing a lot of people.

Before I knew it, I was asked to come in on a Sunday because someone could not come in. The enjoyment made it easier for me to say yes. I guess I was on a roll. The pleasure of having the job I wanted and experiencing promotions weakened my resolve a little. So I decided to do what I had promised I wouldn't do. I worked that one Sunday, and that was it, is what I told myself. Have you noticed that just before compromise comes the phrase, "just this once"? I honestly believed it would be the only time, but I didn't know that I had let my guard down. Proverbs 4:23 says, *"Keep thy heart with all diligence; for out of it are the issues of life."* Unfortunately, I had let the job take root in my heart.

In addition, I was paid weekly, and when I received my check, there was another premium shift pay on there. I asked the manager about it because I didn't want them to take anything out of my next check. But she explained that if you're originally not on the schedule to work and you picked up or filled in, you get another premium. I'm like, okay, that's another plus to this! The next schedule came out, and again, there was an opening for Sunday. I took it! Seen that free tank of gas increase in my check, and I was on a roll. Before I knew it, I worked two to three Sundays a month and picked up on other days. I had extra money to save and treat my daughter more.

Slowly but surely, I was beginning to set my job above my devotion to God. I saw keeping the Sabbath holy as obedience to God. So breaking it now for extra money was a sign that I was worshipping something else. I became too confident in my job because I knew that I would get that extra money if I put in the work on Sundays. Plus, extra money meant I could do things I couldn't do before. But I didn't know the implication of my actions. By doing this, I depended solely on my skill and job. I put God out of the equation of my life. It was no longer about depending on God and trusting in His blessings. If I wanted to get something done with cash, I just had to plan the budget and put in the extra work.

Doesn't the Bible say in Matthew 6:24 (NKJV), *"24 "No one can serve two masters; for either he will hate the one and love the other, or else he will be loyal to the one and despise the other. You cannot serve God and mammon."* By giving the day that belongs to God to work and money, I was serving two masters. In fact, I made my job an idol, and God is a jealous God.

Every Idol Shall Be Destroyed

Isaiah 2:17-18 (NKJV) *"17 The loftiness of man shall be bowed down, And the haughtiness of men shall be brought low; The Lord alone will be exalted in that day, 18 But the idols He shall utterly abolish."*

Whatever you esteem above God is an idol. You don't have to build a graven image and bow before it. Ezekiel 14:3 (NKJV) says, ***"3 "Son of man, these men have set up their idols in their hearts,*** *and put before them that which causes them to stumble into iniquity. Should I let Myself be inquired of at all by them?"* You see, the state of your heart determines whether you're worshipping God. Your idols don't have to be physical objects; they can be in your heart. God wants to be exalted in your life, so everything that consumes your heart will be destroyed. Indeed, no matter what it is, anything that takes God's place in your life is an idol. And just as the above scripture reveals, God will destroy every idol.

Your heart is a space that only God should occupy. As a result, destruction comes on anything you esteem above God. I Samuel 5:1-7 gives a graphic picture of what happens to anything that tries to share space with God:

"1 Then the Philistines took the ark of God and brought it from Ebenezer to Ashdod. 2 When the Philistines took the ark of God, they brought it into the temple of Dagon and set it by Dagon. 3 And when the people of Ashdod arose early in the morning, there was Dagon, fallen on its face to the earth before the ark of the Lord. So they took Dagon and set it in its place again. 4 And when they arose early the next morning, there was Dagon, fallen on its face to the ground before the ark of the Lord. The head of Dagon and both the palms of its hands were broken off on the threshold; only Dagon's torso was left of it. 5 Therefore neither the priests of Dagon nor any who come into Dagon's house tread on the threshold of Dagon in Ashdod to this day. 6 But the hand of the Lord was heavy on the people of Ashdod, and He

ravaged them and struck them with tumors, both Ashdod and its territory. 7 And when the men of Ashdod saw how it was, they said, "The ark of the God of Israel must not remain with us, for His hand is harsh toward us and Dagon our god."

The Philistines didn't know the God they dealt with. The fact that they could put another god in the house of God shows that only God is holy. There is none like Him; God is high and set apart. Just as He couldn't share that space with Dagon, He can't share your heart with idols.

Did you notice what happened to the image of Dagon? It was destroyed, signifying that God's presence had destroyed the God of the Philistines. The same thing happens to the things we allow to compete with God's sovereignty and Lordship in our lives.

When the Philistines saw their God in pieces, they were shocked but didn't quickly discern what had happened. It took them time to understand that God is supreme, and no god can exist in His presence. Have you esteemed anything in your heart above God? What has taken God's place? Are you sensitive enough to understand that the crisis in your life is the destruction of idols?

Friend, if there's anything you hold dear that has become greater than God, demote it while there's still time. From experience, God will curse a business, job, or anything that acts as a god in your life. He has commanded in His Word, *"You shall have no other gods before me."* (Exodus 20:3 NKJV)

In my case, my job became an idol, and I had to face the music. You see, God can turn against something He gave as a blessing because you've set it above Him. About four months later, we were in the office, and the lead kitchen manager entered with a look on her face I had never seen before. She took a chair from a desk no one was sitting at and sat in the aisle way where everyone could see her. She called three other women's names in the office and told them they could take their break. As they walked out, four other kitchen workers came in and sat down. I never once looked right or left to see if anyone else was curious as I was. She stated that the hospital needed to make some emergency cuts in the budget and that we were being laid off for an INDEFINITE period.

I now look around like what the heck just happened here. Finally, I find something I like, and it's being taken away from me. It was given and now taken away. They brought in the HR representative to explain unemployment benefits, gave us all this paperwork, and said we no longer have a job for you. Have a nice life!

Don't Fall for the Money Trap

During my drive home, the sun seemed to be shining so hard. After I took in how things happened, I knew that I had abused the blessing that was run by my fear and distrust that He will provide for us whether I work on Sunday or not as long as I follow His commandments. Also, I had a lack of discipline to stand on what I knew. I fell into the money trap!

God doesn't want His children to be ruled by material desires. He wants you to completely depend on Him for your needs. Now, this doesn't mean God supports idleness. On the contrary, you've seen that God loves work. But it's not His will that His children work for money. As a believer, you make choices about your job and career based on God's purpose and guidance. Yes, you don't work the highest-paying job because of the paycheck.

Have you wondered why Adam worked the Garden? It wasn't because He needed to make ends meet. Adam worked in the Garden because God asked Him to do it. Keeping and dressing the Garden was God's will for Him.

Another question to ask is, how did Adam and Eve survive? Well, God gave them access to every tree in the Garden except the tree of the knowledge of good and evil. Therefore, they were prosperous and successful. Indeed, if you follow this template for your life, you won't fall into the trap of chasing money. God wants you to seek His kingdom and His righteousness. Material things ought to come as additions to the believer that is on God's assignment.

Therefore, if those who seek God's kingdom will experience an increase, those who chase after material things will reduce. Do you know what the Bible says about chasing money? Proverbs 23:4-5 (NIV) says, *"Do not wear yourself out to get rich: do not trust your own cleverness. Cast but a glance at riches, and they are gone, for they will surely sprout wings and fly off to the sky like an eagle."*

When you chase wealth, it will elude you. But when you chase God, He'll make wealth chase you and serve you. Chase me? *Yes,* Deuteronomy 28:1-2 (NKJV) says, *"1 "Now it shall come to pass, if you diligently obey the voice of the Lord your God, to observe carefully all His commandments which I command you today, that the Lord your God will set you high above all nations of the earth. **2 And all these blessings shall come upon you and overtake you, because you obey the voice of the Lord your God.***" Did you notice the word "Overtake?" It means you can't escape being blessed when you love God and serve Him with all your heart.

When I fell for the money trap, I disobeyed God's command to keep the Sabbath holy, and as a result, I lost God's blessings. I started trusting the job more than God and depended on it to give me a good life. The good news is, even when I lost that job, I got better opportunities and achieved greater things. Don't ever fall for the money trap because money can't sustain you; only God can.

God Wants You to Experience Rest

Hebrews 3:11 says, *"11 So I swore in My wrath, 'They shall not enter My rest."* These words were spoken concerning the children of Israel. During the time of their Exodus from Egypt, they disbelieved God and murmured against Him. He showed them great signs, expecting them to believe in Him, but they didn't.

Through faith, God wanted them to enter supernatural rest. That is, God wanted them to cease from their work and efforts; He wanted to work on their behalf. Yet, they refused and turned against God.

You might not be as rebellious as the Israelites, but your worry and self-dependence stop God from stepping into your life. To experience God's rest, you must cease from your works. Beyond observing the Sabbath, God wants you to focus your heart on Him. He wants you to enjoy His abundance and take part in His victories.

Isaiah 30:15-16 (NKJV) says, *"15 For thus says the Lord God, the Holy One of Israel: "In returning and rest you shall be saved; In quietness and confidence shall be your strength." But you would not, 16 And you said, "No, for we will flee on horses"-- Therefore you shall flee! And, "We will ride on swift horses"-- Therefore those who pursue you shall be swift!* Have you behaved like the persons in this text? God said, "Rest," but you worked. God said, "trust," but you doubted. Or did God say, "I'll handle it," and you said, "how?" God is giving you a second chance today. He wants you to live a life of rest. Replace anxieties and struggles with peace by trusting God with your work and every area of your life.

Chapter 5:

I WILL honor You

(Honor your father and your mother, that your days may be long upon the earth)

Dear Sweetie,

I had a long day yesterday. I worked so hard with you in mind. This is a difficult situation, but I have to keep you in a safe place, under the radar, and guarded. Your parents are extremely disappointed and ashamed of you. I hope they do not consider putting you out on the streets. You will be a mother at seventeen, well, eighteen years old, two days after the due date.

You know, *Guilt* and I will always aim to keep the spotlight off of you. Honey, you are always on my mind. I remember when we first met. It was after you found out you were pregnant; you began to hide it from everyone. You hid it with denial, in me, Fear. You would always come to me when you're in doubt, shame, and insecurity. I will shield you, tuck you away. You can't count on anyone else but me. Everyone is and will judge you, talk about you, and dissect your shortcomings. Where is that good God when you need Him? See, I will never let you go! Even your friends *Joy* and *Hope* left you in your time of need. I just can't understand how God is working all things for your good, yet He stood still and allowed all these things to happen?

You can't tell me Mr. All-knowing didn't see this coming! You are the 3rd generation in your family that this has happened to. But the love I have for you will see us through. We're going to build these walls and chains to keep everyone and everything out from the "you" I see. I am thankful and so happy that I am with you.

Love, Fear

Another Life to Live

What's the worst thing you've ever done? I mean something that really affected your life in a bad way. Certainly, everybody has something they're not too proud of. But imagine living with the consequences of your mistakes for a long time. My mistake was getting pregnant out of wedlock—as a teenage girl. But when I refer to the consequences, I'm not talking about my daughter— she's the blessing God gave me from a bad situation. Rather, I refer to the stigma of making such a public mistake. You see, God works everything out for good, a way maker. Before we go any further, I want you to go about life expecting God to turn things around. I will stand to testify that He can take the blindness of sins and turn it into the sight of blessings.

I can remember clear as day, January 1, 2003, was when my life took a turn at the age of seventeen. What a way to usher in the New Year, right? My mom, brother, and I were heading back from Ohio after my aunt's funeral. I had gotten an allergic reaction to an over-the-counter drug I had taken for what seemed like the flu. The rash had covered my entire body, which kept me up all night. So we headed back home and stopped at a Med Express. That is where we found out that I was about four and a half months pregnant. That was the quietest and longest ride home ever. We get home, and thankfully, my mom chose to tell my dad. The throat-cutting silence continued even longer.

When Hope Is Shattered

Have you ever stumbled on the story of a young lady called Dinah in the bible? What caused the silence of her name through the entire pages of the scripture after Genesis 34? I mean, Dinah happens to be the only daughter of Jacob. She was the single lady among several brothers—12 of them. Obviously, God had glorious plans for her, but something happened that silenced her and made her into a secluded and fearful being.

Not only that, but she also brought disgrace to her clan in Israel. When young girls go all out hooking up with ungodly friends, they seem not to often think of any other person who may be affected by their wrong decisions and the result of their gullible lifestyle. You see, I never understood or gave thought to the pain my early pregnancy would bring my parents. Think about the stigma in society.

Dinah was blessed with the heritage of living to become a great part of the patriarchs, but her place became history because she was defiled. In our world today, it's becoming increasingly hard and not fashionable to stay pure and undefiled.

Genesis 34:1-2 revealed the beginning of the stigma Dinah carried till she died. It was quite unfortunate that Dinah couldn't get over the effect of her act of negligence. Look what happened to Dinah here: *"Now Dinah the daughter of Leah, whom she had borne to Jacob, went out to see the daughters of the land. And when Shechem the son of Hamor the Hivite, prince of the country, saw her, he took her and lay with her, and violated her.*

You see, I have come to realize that no decision made will go with any effect on the fabric of our personality. This effect could either be positive or negative. Dinah left the comfort of her home where her protection was guaranteed, falling into place where sexually hungry men were domicile. Shechem defiled her.

We seem to be so passionate about doing what we want during our tender age that we walk proudly into situations that humble us and leave our heads bowed in pity. That was my experience! My unwanted pregnancy really humbled me and left me confused at some point. I wished I could turn back the hands of the clock and rewrite my narrative. But then, the ink of time is made with permanent sceneries.

Dinah's case brought shame not only on her but also on her family. The bible said in Genesis 34:7, *"And the sons of Jacob came in from the field when they heard it; and the men were grieved and very angry, because he had done a disgraceful thing in Israel by lying with Jacob's daughter, a thing which ought not to be done."* They counted the act Dinah engaged herself in as folly! But I will call it the folly of youthfulness. Just like Dinah's experience, I was almost lost in the ocean of my guilt and mistakes; life suffocated peace out of me.

It felt as though I could not breathe nor talk to say anything to save my life, just like nobody asked Dinah what ensued between her and Shechem. Her ugly experience silenced her and made her a being of pity and rejection. Just when I thought life should sprout beauty and play melodious rhythms to me, guilt kept drowning my hope of a better tomorrow. Have you ever found yourself in a spot where your past and present collided in nothingness and hollowness?

The more I attempted to say anything, the more I felt like I had to force myself to breathe. I could not believe this was happening. To be candid, I allowed myself to get caught up in an empty chase after the mirage of fleeting pleasure. I remember being terrified when Brenda started clinching down on her stomach in the bathroom at school while going into labor in Tupac's video; Brenda's Got a Baby. Even the video of "I Miss You" by Aaron Hall started playing in my head when his wife woke up out of her sleep in labor. She ended up dying while having her baby.

Obviously, there are times where we are trapped between a rock and a hard place. It's a place where even death looks appealing, an exit route from the pain our soul is subjected to. Imagine someone like me, totally confused and devoid of peace with several haunting thoughts, kept strolling down the corridors of my mind. That is not a good combination.

Of course, the first thoughts that ran through my head had bad outcomes from having a baby! I had to figure out an exit plan on this one. Do I run away, move out of town with relatives, or get an abortion? Shoot, can I even get an abortion this late in the game? If I move, will my parents help me? It will alleviate some of the embarrassment for them. If I stay gone long enough, people may forget about me. You know, out of sight, out of mind.

Running away, I won't have help, money, or a place to stay. So that option is out of the window. This baby does not deserve to come into this world with teen parents, no roof over her head, and just barely the necessities of life, all because of my dumb mistake. It's not fair! Abortion has a bottom line, if there is no visible belly, no baby, and there's no need for the rest. After about five minutes of that thought, I made about two calls to the abortion clinics nearby. It did not take long for my mind to come back to reality.

Ebony, your parents are already pissed at you for getting pregnant. They're not going for that either! They will most likely throw me out and be disappointed at me for terminating a new life. Would I even be able to live with myself after the abortion? No, I wouldn't! I don't want a baby haunting me in my dreams or anything... maybe I watch too many movies too.

Calling Abortion Its Real Name: Murder!

Think about the world of truth revealed in Jeremiah 1: 5 about the child in the womb. *"Before I formed you in the womb I knew you; Before you were born I sanctified you; I ordained you a prophet to the nations. "* You know, because we refer to the baby in the womb by the word *"it, "* doesn't mean that the seed within you is a thing that can be disposed willfully into the trash can.

Look at what God told Jeremiah in verse above. God said before Jeremiah was born, He has sanctified and anointed him as a prophet to the Israelites. Wow! What an amazing statement. A child that wasn't born into this world already carries a prophetic ordination. What if the mother of Jeremiah disposed of him while in the womb? What if she felt, "oh? I'm not ready to take care of this baby. So, I better do away with him." Who do you think she will be killing? A prophet of God.

What you think is a lifeless entity that could be aborted is a gift of God to his generation. Imagine if Moses had been killed from the womb; who has Mama Jochebed killed? The God-sent deliverer of the Israelites from captivity in Egypt. Folks, you must be careful not to make a big mistake in terminating such a precious gift to you and this earth.

One story always baffles me in the scriptures. It's the story of Rebekah's pregnancy experience. See how God described the seeds in her: *"Now Isaac pleaded with the LORD for his wife, because she was barren; and the LORD granted his plea, and Rebekah his wife conceived. But the children struggled together within her; and she said, "If all is well, why am I like this?" So she went to inquire of the LORD. And the LORD said to her: "Two nations are in your womb, Two peoples shall be separated from your body; One people shall be stronger than the other, And the older shall serve the younger." So when her days were fulfilled for her to give birth, indeed there were twins in her womb."*- Genesis 25:21-24

How did God describe the babies in the womb of Rebekah? God called them *two nations.* Wow! That unborn child means a lot to God. God sees the end in the beginning. Abortions come from fear, a lack of faith. That is why the enemy wants to convince women to have abortions because it makes his job easier to destroy us.

So, I knew abortion wasn't an option at all. I lay in my bed, rubbing my stomach, crying as quietly as I could even though my bedroom door was shut. All that I could do was say I'm sorry over and over with the circular motion as I rubbed my stomach. My lips were just moving, no voice, but I could hear myself in my head, hoping that the baby and I are connected enough that she could hear it too:

"I'm sorry, I'm sorry, I'm so sorry for what I'm about to put
you through, the life that I am about to give you. I am not
married, nor am I with your father. I am still a child myself and

don't have any real-life experiences to share with you yet. I'm sorry that we're going to grow up together. My perspective on certain things will mature or change, seeing things one way now and learning better later. I may miss some opportunities in the midst of me learning myself. We will then have to redefine who we are as young ladies together. It's going to be hard as ever sometimes not to want to be your friend instead of your mother, which will lead to more mistakes. I will have trust issues because we're so close in age that I can quickly step back and place my feet in your shoes. I want better for you than the tunnel that's ahead. I'm sorry baby, that there will be moments of selfishness from me being so young and not mature yet. I hate that I can't say I was ready for this. I can say I will do the best I know to do and be the best to see you through. It's easy to see the darkness and the clouds from afar, but you can't when it's right over you and happening. But through whatever is ahead, just know that you will be one of my biggest achievements. I'm going to love you the best way that I know how. I'm going to push you to be better and do better. I'm sorry that I will hand you a heavy torch to carry to the finish line. It is needed to break this family from bondage of a generational curse. This has happened to your nana, your aunt, and now your mother; you have to break through this and make it to the starting line of adulthood, unlike us. At least to the point in your life where you're spiritually rooted, financially independent and stable, experienced life, and gotten to know yourself. Unfortunately, I'm about to hang off this cliff for you, to build a bridge to another side of life I won't get to experience. That's the least I can do for what you are about to endure. I love you, whoever you are, my baby…"

At that point, I knew I only had one option, to give birth to this baby. I know I can't do this without my mom's help. I'm not fooling anybody, not even myself. This leaves me nothing, just to put my big girl panties on and endure. I allowed this to happen, so I must deal with what's to come on my end. From that moment forward, I realized my life had changed forever. So, I went ahead and got my first job at McDonald's to start. Before I knew it, I was at my first ultrasound appointment, finding out that IT'S A GIRL! I also decided not to force myself to move out; I'd rather stay home with my parents, so I won't risk having to struggle to make ends meet if I were to move out with the baby.

The Walk of Shame

During my pregnancy, the lies they told had begun, and the carpet had rolled out for the walk of shame. Indeed, shame is an unpleasant emotion. Being a teenage mother, I got acquainted with the same. It was there when I woke up every morning. Wherever I went, shame was there, trailing my steps. It was like a dark cloud over my life.

I expected I'll be the topic of discussion amongst my peers, but not from adults with no direct relation or connection to me. It even affected my parents at church, the positions they held, with so-called friends and family. This showed me a whole different perspective on so-called adults, people, and life in general. The world is cold, and if you don't get thick skin to warm up quickly, you will freeze to death.

My mistakes didn't only impact negatively on my life and my baby's life, but also on others' lives as well. I never wanted that. It drove me to feel like a failure. My self-esteem went down the drain, but I rarely showed it; no one was aware of it. God, where are you? Why punish my parents for my mistakes? What good is this going to bring? I felt bad for my mom. She would defend me, but she wouldn't tell me what was happening. I wanted to set some folks straight; I needed them to stop provoking my mom.

Things may get hard, and we may get down but move out of the way when we rise to the occasion. Unexpectedly for them, I made it through senior year, graduated, and beat the odds of that. My baby girl (in my belly) and I walked across that stage, and we went to the prom. One month later, I was able to put my eyes on my daughter. Seeing her gave me a reason to live. She was now my "Why." I fell in love but feeling bad for her at the same time. Real-life is here, here to stay; there's no turning back now.

Summer of 2003, I watched some friends head off to college, dorm rooms, having open houses, and here I am, bringing a baby into the world. I could tell people expected me to be the typical teen mom, have more kids, no education, work to make ends meet, and depend on public assistance. The ghetto bird in the grocery store with five kids yelling out loud, "Get your big head over here" or "Stop touching stuff" or "... "looking just like your daddy!" NO NO NO NO! So to avoid being a repeat offender, I got on "the shot."

The Depo Provera was the savior back then! I would watch the TV show "Teen Mom" on MTV. I figured, if it's on TV, it's drama, so do the total opposite. I didn't want to amount to anything like everyone expected. I needed to level up, not just for me, my baby, and now my parents as well. As time went by, I hadn't had any more kids and had raised my income from $5.15 to $10.35 within six years. That was a decent raise I gave myself back then. Some folks got raises of .30 per year.

When I acquired a job, I didn't stop applying, I applied for jobs higher in pay than what I was making. In between there, I worked retail, in a medical facility, and nursing home. My daughter was now almost six years old. I had always kept a nice car, was now making decent money to manage off of, and was almost ready to move out. I took classes in college but was never 100% satisfied with what I chose to major in. My major probably changed four times, at least. It went from psychology to criminal justice, business, sonography, and then to nursing from what I remember.

By now, my classmates from high school are graduating from college, moving out of the state, and getting married. I had none of that anywhere close to my radar. That was beginning to bother me, especially with school. I wanted to graduate, get a good job, and provide a nice life for me and mine. It all hit hard when I had maxed out my hourly wage with my job.

Do you mean to tell me my pay won't be increasing any time soon? It's time to hit the internet and start back applying again. I was starting to like that job, but I chose to pursue an LPN certification at a school close to two hours away for one consistent year. During that time, my daughter would stay with my parents. I found a place, and a job, then I got enrolled at the school and was ready to make that move.

One week before I was supposed to move down there, the job fell through. I had to make the landlord aware of what happened, and she graciously gave my deposit back. There was someone else wanting to rent it right away. Now once again, I'm stuck here! God must still be upset with me. Every effort to advance becomes a failed mission. I need to take matters into my own hands and push through because He has left me hanging. I had already quit my job.

Full of pride, I did not want to return to my old job to ask for my position back. I was too embarrassed that the plan had flopped. I attempted to find work elsewhere, but it appeared that my job-hopping luck had run out. During my internet search, I ran across an advertisement for the Navy. Yes, the military is what I'm referring to. I can earn and learn, have an established career, make decent money, retire in twenty years, and get my lazy butt in shape! This appeared to be a no-lose situation.

However, the downfall was the thought of leaving my daughter for three months, states away, and being yelled at in my face. If you yell in my face, be prepared to be yelled at or maybe worse under any other circumstances! In a desperate position, I went to speak with a recruiter. Officer Daniels was cool and convinced that I could do it. He set a date for me to take the practice ASVAB. The test showed I could go in as an E3 with those scores, which was good to me. My weight was good, and my physical health was fairly good too. I was excited about the fact that this could be a serious possibility.

At my next meeting with Officer Daniels, he went over some of the job options I was interested in and explained some other technicalities. My daughter was also a topic of discussion. Long story short, I was not interested in putting my name on any paper stating that I'm giving up my rights as her biological parent. I didn't care that it was temporary. I just didn't feel right; that's just me. I commend all of the single mothers who did what they had to do. I just didn't feel that that's what I needed to do at that time.

So now I'm back to square one! The next route I chose to pursue was, enroll in college instead of vocational schooling, not my preferred method, but it led to the same outcome. I started taking classes and continued searching for part-time work at least. I saw a part-time position for students in my search, which would give me a $3 raise from my last job and was a state government agency. This appeared to be too good to be true, but what would I lose by still applying besides crushed hopes. You know I had to go for it, couldn't help myself.

Two days later, my phone is ringing, and I answer the unknown phone number. It was the supervisor for the "fake position" I applied for! I was so shocked; I even had the nerve to tell her that I thought the position wasn't real. She thought that was hilarious and seen the drive for me to still apply. Let's just say she liked our conversation, gave me an interview, and hired me! This was my open door to getting in with the State.

I will take that. I started there as a student assistant with no benefits in 2010. I had finally begun accumulating the income I needed to move out of my parents' home. By November, I had moved into my first apartment. The following year I was promoted to a State position with full benefits, raises every six months, and purchased my first home as a single mother at the age of twenty-six. And yes, I still only had one daughter. One of my main concerns outside of my child and her well- being, is my parents proud now? Not that they never told me, but that I didn't end up how the typical would. Through all of this, I just needed to honor my parents for seeing me through. God also gets the glory and honor when we are obedient!

Chapter 6:

I WILL focus on You
(You shall not commit murder)

Hey Honey

Let me start by saying I am glad that I found you. I could not have grown if it were not for you. You let me in, and we have been rocking and rolling since. Sometimes, I don't hear from you for a while, but I know our love will find its way back to each other. I saw how overwhelmed you were and wanted to help. I brought *Empty* with me to help take your mind off of things. We can have a spa day. I will massage your mind first, and then I'll have her massage your heart and soul.

This will give us more time together to enjoy each other. If I'm with you, we can live in your past, present, and future together. That's what I want for us. Initially, the massage will hurt a little, but it will be a little smoother as we smash down the knots. You know, we can't totally get rid of them; it's just build-up that we smooth out. As long as it doesn't get too big, we can keep it inside. She makes room for other things to have space in those areas. You don't have to worry about being complacent; you'll always be looking for more things to do and make happen.

You will be busy sometimes. Always be sure you are dressed for success, if nothing else, and you'll be good. Your beauty is so enchanting that you must always look good. I am in bliss when I see you and when I'm with you. Honestly, I show you the real you, especially your challenges. But I love being with you through it all to show you who you are in trials and that I will always step in and choose you. It's okay to be angry, frustrated, depressed, and insecure because I am here to be there with you. No one can tell you when to come out of it.

I aim to be the piece that's missing in your puzzle. Your mind intertwines us. Our chemistry is perfect together. I intervene when your weaknesses are being highlighted. I am the sugar in your Kool-Aid, the bacon with your eggs, and the ketchup on your fries. Can you tell I'm hungry? I'm hungry for more of you. I'm going to leave Empty here with you while I go to find some "whole" foods to eat.

Love, Fear

Lose Myself to Gain Perspective

I lost myself at the age of eighteen, trying to catch up with the life I had placed myself in and not realizing I hadn't had time to get to know myself. At the beginning of the prior year, I didn't have a care in the world besides my selfish teenage concerns. The next year, I have someone else's life as my responsibility. I couldn't be myself because I had to make parental decisions that seemed exaggerated to my age but were sensible and mature to my situation.

I was extremely uncomfortable, and from time to time, I felt sorry for myself and hated myself at the same time behind closed doors. Someone slowly died inside of me over time as I had to mature faster than my peers. It wasn't until I got married that it became more apparent that inadequacy was a battle for me.

Inadequacy is a spiritual fight that occurs when your old self tries to take the lead ahead of your future self.

~Ebony White

When It All Began

It started in the dating stage of our relationship. Abe has always been a lover, a friend, a brother, and a support through my rough and challenging times. I would follow his example of how to display my love and appreciation for him. But as I began to realize there were things I didn't know about myself, it became more difficult over time.

Abe was too good to be true. I could see the love, respect, affection, attention, and all from him. He was and is ambitious, optimistic, and loves to challenge me to be better. But I allowed my downfalls to dictate the final say. He saw so much in me that I could not see within myself. That's where I began to see it's difficult to be the woman he needed because I didn't know myself enough to know who I needed him to be. He believed in me more than I did in myself. I began to feel as though I didn't deserve to be with him. But then there were days I felt as though I would lose myself even more if I just became everything he wanted me to be.

Somebody else has it all put together better than me, so I began to act out in ways that pushed him away sometimes. The more I pushed him away, the farther he got. There were days when I would be distant, communication was limited, and I was moody. These days became more frequent after we got married; I felt inadequate because he knew what he needed, and it seemed to be a bit too much for me to handle.

Abe is a strong man, and his strength, which I used to love to hide myself in, became a constant torment for me. It was a constant reminder of my weakness and fragility, and I wouldn't say I liked it. I detested Abe for constantly reminding me of it, and I felt insufficient for not being the strong woman he needed me to be. My inability to believe in myself made me disbelieve his confessions of love and even suspect his affectionate display of support.

When we fail to love ourselves for who we are, we find it difficult to let someone else love us. Your imperfections and mistakes make you human and lead you to become better and grow into the understanding of the importance of God in erasing and redeeming your past, but I failed to see this. I characterized my life around a mistake I made in my teenage years, though it's not erasable, but workable.

Meeting Abe pricked a sensitive part of me I'd try to hide and accept, but his unconditional love left my fears in the open and my insecurities irrelevant. I tried to measure up to his love and acceptance by creating the *me* I felt he deserved to have. Still, Abe always had his way of bringing out the vulnerable side of me and making me try to love him as he did, but things didn't play out well.

Abe and I met at our job in 2011. I was in a rough spot in my life where my self-esteem was nil, and my self-confidence lost. Unexpectedly, meeting him sparked something inside of me I wanted to unravel. He didn't want me because of my outfit or body shape. He called me beautiful, yet he never starred at me lustfully. I wanted to see more of him, but I also didn't like to be treated as a charity case.

Despite my inner battles with myself, I couldn't help but give in to his requests for outings. Abe was a gentleman and never tried; neither did he initiate any sexual advances towards me. I was intrigued by this and offended. My desire to make him perceive me as someone worthy of him led me to do things I didn't have to. Unnecessary decisions fueled by a misdirected desire to be seen and appreciated. I loved the way Abe looked at me like I was something valuable and precious. I wanted to please him by being the woman he thought of me to be.

I stopped using make-up for a while because I wanted to feel beautiful, but that was a battle I'd lost a long time ago. Make-up had become my shield against the world. It covered my scars well and made me invincible. My face without make-up exposed more than I could handle. I wasn't ready for the world to see that part of me yet, and I love that Abe didn't force me. He understood my struggles and offered his help in the bits I was ready for.

Inadequacy can make you feel less than who you are. You're forced to carry yourself lesser than your worth and value. I didn't understand that everyone was just moving in the way they thought was right, and not all the people I admired had it figured out.

My dates with Abe were wonderful, and I loved that someone could see me in a different light. In the light, I'd always longed to be seen in--as necessary. Every date left me craving for more and feeling as though he could do better. The constant fear of losing Abe, the one person who valued me, became unbearable, and I had to start enforcing excuses to see him or have him compliment me. I drew my strength from his constant compliments. Every "you're beautiful" and "you look good today" was stored up in a box in my heart where I cherished it till it lost its convincing ability to make me believe it.

Inadequacy is like a black hole. You continually pick the beautiful things to fill it up, but the more you throw them in, the more they disintegrate into thin age like they never even existed, leaving the dark hole growing deeper and wider. I looked to Abe to find a cure for my ailment of lack of self-worth. I believed I could redefine myself through his love and receive healing by his words, but the more I leaned on him to determine my self-value, the more confused, worthless and depressed I became.

Friend, no man or woman can heal you from the feeling of inadequacy. It is a conscious decision to be better in your own eyes. The best way to heal is to first believe in your divine predestination as a child of God. Most people know something about God; they attend church services regularly but always find it difficult to believe in God's love for them. That was similar to my case too. I wrestled with my mistakes so much that I began to define myself by them. I believed no one could love me because of my mistakes and how low I esteemed myself.

No one will honor you if you lack honor for yourself. I admired the way Abe looked at me and introduced me to his friends. I always looked forward to us running into one of Abe's friends or colleagues. I had the concept of value all wrong. I never perceived myself as a person of value, so it was not strange that I found it difficult to sustain the tone of Abe's love confessions.

I failed to understand that my past was just that, my past, and should not have a hold on how my future ended. My refusal to deal with the root cause of my problems led me to go against Abe and blame him for his standards which I felt were too high for me to reach, and his expectations I just couldn't picture for myself.

Suicide first starts from the mind losing hope for redemption. Then it leads to self-pity, then depression, and ultimately loss of life. I wallowed in my inability to wake up from my self-deception. Inadequacy or low self-esteem is mostly birthed from the deception that you're no better than anyone else. You continuously find a place to fit into, and even when you find your spot, you'll fail to recognize it, just as you've been unable to recognize your uniqueness and beauty. Truth is, you can't be like everyone else because everyone else is taken. You have to be yourself, and until you begin to see yourself for your awesomeness, you'll never be able to add that value you are ordained to contribute to your relationship, family, and society.

That was my mistake, failing to see my errors as a pointer to becoming a better person and not living by anyone's standard. Truth is, you'll never meet everyone's standard for you. Even if you try to, you will become a foreign manifestation of who you are.

Here are four scriptural passages to shut the door of your heart to the increasing flood of bad experiences of the past: read and confess these verses to yourself each time those thoughts of inadequacy and past failures come to sweep you off your feet.

- ➤ **Philippians 3:13**—*"Brethren, I do not count myself to have apprehended; but one thing I do, forgetting those things which are behind and reaching forward to those things which are ahead"*
- ➤ **Isaiah 43:18-19**—*"Do not remember the former things, Nor consider the things of old. Behold, I will do a new thing, Now it shall spring forth; Shall you not know it? I will even make a road in the wilderness And rivers in the desert."*
- ➤ **Hebrews 10:17**—*"then He adds, "Their sins and their lawless deeds I will remember no more."*
- ➤ **Romans 8:1**—*"There is therefore now no condemnation to those who are in Christ Jesus,* who do not walk according to the flesh, but according to the Spirit."*

Take each of these verses like divine injections packed with divine life to transfer joy and vitality into your full inner being. Instead of covering up your sense of inadequacy and low self-esteem, why not apply Peter's little faith and step out of your fearful boat to walk on the ocean of life, in spite of the storm of discouragement, while you fix your gaze on the rock of ages.

Never leave a false perception to meet a man or woman. I mean, imagine a woman who met a man in the club. She was all dressed up, face beat (make-up done nicely), hair done, nails done, and her feet too. She may have girdled up and put on her best pushup bra. He loved what he saw; she's looking like a celebrity. They exchange numbers and plan to see each other again. The phone conversation initially is about how beautiful she was and is. Now, that leads her to feel the need to go to that extent every time they see each other. It begins to be too much for her, but she continues to do it to see him She wants to keep up the persona she originally gave. There was an attempt to go without make-up. When she removed it to show her natural beauty because she was tired, she didn't like what she had seen. Her natural had been neglected for so long that it needed some things to resolve some issues that she had buried under the layers of cover-up.

It is okay to smile while you're going through, just don't ignore what you're going through, while you smile.

~Ebony White

For a man or a woman, you need to bring your best self to a relationship. No need for pretense! A man that cannot take you or love you for who you are is not worthy of you. Many stumble into a relationship with little or no knowledge of who they're in a relationship with. So, getting into the marriage, they were grandly welcome by disheartening experiences.

It is particularly important to know who you're in a relationship with. Knowing yourself along with your mate will alleviate a lot of disagreements, distrust, and feelings of not being enough. Do you remember what the Bible said in Amos 3:3? It says, *"Can two walk together, unless they are agreed?"* This agreement must be in thought, worldview, and perspective to life's likes and dislikes. But then, none of this really hit me until he had expressed to me that he didn't know what else to do to make me happy.

He was blaming himself for the predicament that I put myself in and chose not to get myself out of. I thought that I was punishing just myself when it was making him feel helpless. When I sit back and think about how bad I wanted to relive and "correct" my past, it's almost as though I killed myself internally. You see, I believe that self-esteem is one of those precious things you need that you can't buy. It should be seen as self-care, not self-destruction. Therefore, that is why Emerson said, *"What lies behind us and what lies before us are tiny matters compared to what lies within us."*

My internal should be my place of peace, not my place of persecution. I lost hope, true joy, happiness, and confidence in myself. I grabbed on and didn't let go of what other people were saying about me. Not once did I consult with myself and take inventory of what I truly knew about myself. The more I ran through my "shoulda coulda wouldas," the more I was disappointed in myself, the more I felt behind in life, the more I felt there were things that I missed out on.

In turn, this all led me to be self-sabotaging. Dwelling on my oppositions was the gun used to commit my own murder. My thoughts and feelings about myself can make or break me. I became so in tuned with negativity. And the Bible plainly reveals that *"For as he thinks in his heart, so is he.",* Proverbs 23:7. Can you see the gravity of what a distorted view of your individuality can internalize? When you think like a defeated fellow, you will act the same way. Even though bad or evil thoughts don't look like suicide. Yet, it's a form of murder; it is just that this is done on the battlefield of your mind. So, believe in yourself and make up your mind to be all that God has ordained you to be through the good, bad, and ugly. Focus on God!

Chapter 7

I WILL be loyal to You
(You shall not commit adultery)

Good morning,

Sweetheart, you are the freshness that inhabits my morning and the peaceful breeze that swirls through my evening. You are what I think about, first thing in the morning, and you're the last thought that lingers on my heart at night. Even though it seems no one will carry you through life when you need it, I promise to walk through life with you– together. No one loves you as I do. I want for you the greatest happiness there could ever be, and I will always be there to make you smile whenever you're down.

I want us to take vacations, go shopping, and not worry about the bills at home. And you know to do that, we have to work extremely hard. Having money opens up so many possibilities; that's why we always need more. We should work more to earn more, baby! I don't know why Abe is even tripping. He knows what it means to work hard for results! Why is he coming down on you? You are a woman of strength, power, and independence. That is why you're special; your guts, firmness, and hardworking quality are what most women lack.

Yes, you may be married, but it's 2019, almost 2020, you need some independence. Marriage isn't imprisonment, isn't that what they say? The fact that you got married to him doesn't mean you shouldn't make the best out of yourself. You are an individual and need to make a name for yourself. You need to carve out your own legacy story. Abe probably wants you to be recognized as his wife, not as the real you– Ebony. He wants to block out your shine, so he fumes about your work. What's wrong with wanting greatness and working for it? And he has to understand you have to keep working so you can be emotionally and mentally stable as well.

He's been in and out of the hospital, so *Unbalanced* wants you to stay busy to not fall off. I would only tell you this because I love you, but you must have something of your own. You shouldn't stop working, so you won't regret it later. Understand that you can't fully depend on him. You have a life of your own. Who knows, he may not always be around, or just in case things don't work out for some reason. I just want you to look at the reality of life. Even though you're supposedly one now because you've been unified, you still have your individuality. And that means you both still have different identities. So, make yours known! Don't lead in the shadow of anyone; you're worth more than that.

You're much more unique than that. I wish we had several lifetimes together because I would spend each one with you. Your mind is the loveseat for my being. I just sink in and relax. With me by your side, you don't need to worry. You can trust me; I have vowed to stay with you for as long as life will give. I see you like a precious gem that I shouldn't let go of. We work great together, I'm here for you, and I want to continue to help you become strong-willed so that you can stand tall.

I learn something new with you every day. If Abe can't see your potential, then you should know that I am right here, with deep insight. I know much about you, and I've always seen this spark of greatness and might in you. Now, you just have to turn this spark into a forest fire; you need to be fueled! You need understanding at this time in your life, not fussing. And I hope you know that if no one else understands you, I do. If no one supports you, look right by your side, and you'll find me firmly and deeply rooted there. I'm always smiling and encouraging you to go after what you want. You're doing your best, and I see you succeed in your next goal. We just need to push a little harder. And work a little harder. Just watch me and listen to what I tell you. Keep your ears tuned into my voice. I will hold your hand and guide your step to walk you through.

Love, Fear

A Shawl for Weakness

The type of person I am, I would be all in or nothing. Financially, we made mistakes, but once a light bulb turned on, we saw the mistakes and put in the work to fix them. I decided to get extra hours at work, so we would make up for the financial mistakes we'd made. While fixing them, I became addicted to the extra workload I took on. In my selfish bid to satisfy my desires by escaping the realities of my weakness, I decided to fill the void growing bigger in my heart with work. The weaknesses I had, I decided to ignore by getting myself occupied and busy with work. I poured myself all into my job; I took it as what could help me get successful and happy. I saw my resources as the sources, wrong! So, that led to me making moves that were no longer beneficial to me and to my home.

Even though we'd planned right in the beginning, I could work so we'd be financially fine; I took it beyond what Abe and I discussed. The solution we'd planned turned out to trap me. They began to be a hindrance versus help. But this was after I recognized that I quit too easily, so I drowned myself in it even deeper and harder. I saw it as a means of escape from that frustrating habit of quitting I had. Since I thought my working hard was a change from what I'd always disliked about me, I was eager and happy to put in all of my best. I saw my unnecessary obsession as becoming more and more engaged in my work.

I was excited about the new ideas I was working on to enhance my production and productivity. I worked 12-hours a day, brought work home with me, and worked most weekends. You should know what this means; it left me no space for other things or people. My work figuratively swallowed me; it was all that preoccupied my head and time. All I could talk about were my ideas, how they were growing, the things I was using them for, money, and where this part of my career was heading. My work consumed me, and Abe was beginning to feel left out and resentful.

In general, he supported me and was proud of me for stepping up, proud of my accomplishments, my sense of industriousness, and my drive. But I had no energy left for him and our girls; I'd given everything to what I later recognized as energy-sapping. Every time we went out, I talked about my other businesses, how they were doing, the life I wanted, and the legacy I wanted to leave. I seldom asked how he was doing if he wanted to talk about anything and never seemed to think about maintaining our relationship anymore. I even stopped doing small, nice things for my husband.

Abe was ready to pump the brakes because my commitment was to the grind. I had pushed him to the wall, and he didn't hide that from me. Not to mention, he was in and out of the hospital during this time too. So, I was not only grinding out of fear with his sickness; I was establishing a relationship with my work, which meant that I was putting my marriage to Abe in serious jeopardy.

The longer I stayed at my job, the farther Abe and I got. I can say it was then a one-sided marriage because I was more committed to my work than I was to him. As there was less important communication, the union's foundation and the family began to shake badly. When Abe brought up the issue about my work, I would respond with, 'Don't we have goals to accomplish? How am I wrong by working hard for the family? This is one thing I haven't easily quit, gratefully, and I thought it was a benefit to you as well.'

Abe felt like I was taking him for granted just because he was sick. We had a lot of talks and misunderstandings about how I was soaking myself deep in the ocean of laboring. After a particularly bad argument about this situation, Abe blurted out, "I didn't sign up to be cheated on by no job!" I was furious, surprised, and confused because I had been working so hard. And I had assumed that we could survive the stress and that he understood my reasoning. I thought he was okay with the decision I made and would bear it well. These times were very trying on my relationship with Abe and the family.

A Light of Realization

After a couple of days of limited conversation, we discussed how I could invest time in my work and still have time for family. The discussion helped us plan what I had to give up or let go of to be back with my family and have time for my personal development. I had also realized that I could eliminate some of those days of extra hours with the understanding that I can't be of service to everyone. Besides, I had too much on my plate, and that I needed to reevaluate what was most important and beneficial after God, my marriage and kids.

Ultimately, I saw that I was chasing success at the expense of my family. I was chasing "success", not my dreams or my destiny and passion. And my family and marriage were what I was putting on the line. I had risked losing them. I saw how selfish I was to have neglected what was of the utmost importance and chased after what couldn't even buy the ones I loved the most. I had to rethink and understand the point Abe had been trying to explain to me all those days we argued. And I asked myself, what exactly is my destiny? Is this something I want to do if it takes all of this to succeed in this field and I'm not 100% fulfilled? I was trying to fill a void with work and "stuff."

I realized I was hoping I could forget the emptiness and what was missing inside of me by submerging myself in work. This realization transported me into another realm of constructive thought. It clicked that I did not know what my purpose was on this earth. This was why I was searching for an alternative instead of finding out what it was. You see, there's this hole in the heart you have when you haven't found your purpose and when you haven't started working towards getting it fulfilled. It was this hole I was trying to patch up. I admitted it was true that I like to feel useful, help others, and see them excel. But then, it was crucial that I needed to also manage my time with work more efficiently and effectively once I figured this out.

I was tired of job-hopping, hobby dipping, and testing the waters. I needed to brace up and step in. I needed to know what it was that I was designed for. The constant desire to feel helpful and relevant was a driving force that led to the tearing apart of my home. I began to put myself before everyone else, and I didn't see the damage I was causing my daughters, husband, and home. I selfishly let myself rule, and it blinded me to the havoc I was bringing on my home.

I'd refused to be corrected and see my errors because I felt I've been committed to my family as best as possible. I felt I was helping with what I was doing and that they ought to support me to achieve my dreams also. I'd resented Abe for making me feel like a failure as a wife. I felt he could have done better by acknowledging and appreciating my efforts for the family. I'd felt his constant complaint was selfish. I failed to see my husband and family valued me and wanted more of me.

Life Taught Me

During that incident that almost tore my marriage and family away from me, I was taught lessons by life. I emerged from that episode with a bag load of knowledge and lessons. I saw that most homes had become a shadow of their former enviable self because the wife and mother did not or could not balance her duties as a wife, mother, and employee or employer.

Truth is that the home is the priority of the woman. She was created as a helper to ease the man's burden of responsibility and help him build a stable, solid, secured home. As a wife and mother, I realized that even though I had my passion and mission, my first commitment is my home. My lane crossing over into my husband's, in which I wasn't allowing him to play as much of his role as he could. He was hospitalized or more stationary, so I didn't utilize him as much as I could have.

I let myself forget my duties to my husband. My vow to support him through thick and thin and see him to his best. I made myself an enemy of my home by fighting the very people I should have been protecting.

I let my fears, worries, and anxiety dictate my role to my husband and family. I saw Abe as a stumbling block to my success instead of seeing him as the head. I disrespected his position as a man and a husband. Lord, put me in the direction you want me to be in. I'm tired of trying to figure this out. By that time, COVID 19 pandemic and nationwide lockdown had taken over, leaving me with less to do and more time to invest in my relationship.

It was then I began to understand the essence of family and what my absence had caused in the lives of our daughters. I came to know the efficacy of my role as their mother and how blessed I was with them as children, including Abe. I apologized to my husband and valued my responsibilities as a wife. I saw my duties as a privilege from God and found satisfaction in doing them.

It also gave me the perfect opportunity to mend the hole that was within me. Lockdown caused by the outbreak of COVID'19 was indeed a blessing in disguise. My lockdown experience helped me discovered some new things within myself, my calling, and the new me. I got closer to God as He continually revealed pieces of my life and how He'd used them to teach me to become better. Abe was one of them. My home was restored, and our daughters were happy. I was much happier, and so was Abe.

After the first wave of the lockdown, I began to apply the understanding I'd gotten from my lockdown experience and time with my family to balance my life, family, and work. Now, we have a better understanding and support for each other.

You see, as a wife, your position is first by God and then your husband. That is your purpose. Everything else will flow from that. Your desire to make an impact and make the world remember you should not be the excuse to neglect your primary assignment. In Proverbs 31:11-12, the virtuous woman is introduced as a keeper, a safe haven to her family. Verse 12 says, *"She does him good and not evil All the days of her life."*

The need for balance in the family is important, but the place of priority must not be neglected. As a woman, your goals and aspirations should not be contradictory to your family's well-being. I've learned to hold on to my family despite the hurdles to safeguard my home.

Right then, I realized that my success definition wasn't related to purpose. I thought success was all about working hard, earning much, living in affluence, and making a name of wealth. I was focused on the outside and thought it would give me the fulfilled feeling I'd always wanted inside of me. I didn't understand that I had to look at what was internal, my spiritual legacy, to produce a traditional legacy, the external.

Most times, success isn't what you think of it to be. I learned this lesson the hard way. Success doesn't mean you get separated from the ones you love and who loved you. Success won't take you away from the ones God has given you divine connection with. Success will never divide your home. And success will not draw you away from God's will and purpose for your life. God in my life has taught me much; these lessons have been loyal and rich to my legacy.

Chapter 8:

I WILL give to You
(You shall not steal)

My Soul mate,

I just want to say that I love you just the way you are. They said that you wouldn't amount to much. You were expected to fail. We can't keep harping over this entrepreneurship stuff; it's not for you. I saw past your mistakes and flaws, knowing that you were bigger than the small mess they were trying to make you out to be. You've cried to me at work, in the shower, in your car, and at night. I have praised you, hugged you, and appreciated you for the queen you are to this world even though they can't recognize it.

After speaking with *Inadequate*, going to college is going to make you. You need the education to make you more marketable in whatever you do. That piece of paper will get you job promotions with higher pay. You won't need to figure out your niche in becoming an entrepreneur. It's okay to go the same route as others have. Life isn't new, so don't try to reinvent the wheel. There's no guarantee in the money you get working for yourself. I would rather have a guarantee than take that risk, wouldn't you? Risks are not always a good sign of going into something new. It's best to stay where you're familiar.

You have a family to take care of. That'll require more work than you want to do. If they did it, you can too! Just imagine where you could be if you had a degree, obviously way past where you are now, and you're doing okay. You got it, honey, determination, and just plain smart. You can't educate yourself the way you need to be. We're not going to worry about the student loans; it's just debt. We all die with some debt anyway. When you do get it done, you will now be successful like everyone else, I promise. This economy is not set up for entrepreneurs, LOL! You are smarter than that.

I'm sorry for venting, but this world has come to nonsense. Back to you, I just don't want you to miss out on something that's worth your time. We don't know if tomorrow is promised, and I would want you to be happy with me and the life you can have.

Love, Fear

Knowledge is Acknowledging Truth

As we walk the path of life from childhood into adulthood, deep within us are glorious hopes and high expectations we have nursed that seems not to come through. *A Dream Deferred,* one of the most influential poems of the 20th century by Langston Hughes, explicated the tragedies of a dream and of hope delayed. Hughes raised critical questions on what happens when a dream is deferred: does it dry up like a raisin in the sun? Or fester like a sore—and then run? Does it stink like rotten meat? Or crust and sugar over—like a syrupy sweet? But then, he concluded by asking if it just sags like a heavy load.

Now, I got an associate's degree in 2017. Before that, I was not having a college degree gave me low self-confidence, which landed me in fear of pursuing things and advancing. I just make up for the void I felt strongly within me. Oh! I know you may be thinking. You may be wondering why I would feel less than just for not having a college degree. I know if you were possibly there when I walked through life with that heavy load of unfulfilled desires, you could have called me to a thoughtful discussion and say, "girl, your sense of worth or importance should not be determined by a degree you have, or you don't have. Come on, girl!"

Yes, you're right. But I can only speak for myself and the expectations I have for myself when I explain this. Meanwhile, my father is the only one in my immediate family who has a bachelor's degree. I wanted to be the next person to do so. But just like Hughes explored the possibilities of having an unfulfilled dream, I was there with no assurance if I would ever have a degree.

I had already subjected myself to being a teen mother, and now I haven't completed a college degree. I knew the areas it could benefit me in. It was hard finding something interesting enough to study for four years that I could see myself offering for at least five years or so, that I could find a job in, and that I could significantly make more money than I was currently making. I would start with something and find a flaw in it that I didn't want to deal with or some of the requirements were ridiculous, or like nursing, I didn't meet the requirements.

Attempting psychology, I came to realize that the real money came when you either got your master's degree or Ph.D. I know myself; I do not like school enough to pursue either one of those. It sounds good, but I need to be realistic. We often plunge into needless heartaches because we want to prove a point without being true to ourselves. As a sonographer, I wanted to perform ultrasounds on pregnant women. But I was told that doing that can be boring often, there are limited job opportunities, and you're in the dark a lot of times. Since I fall asleep in the movie theater from time to time, I may not be a good fit for that one either.

I can admit, I love to sleep, but of course, that has changed since then. I even gave criminal justice a try to pursue a job as a child protective services worker to help children in need. Once I started working for the State, I quickly realized that I do not have the patience or tact needed to maintain my job and deal with the parents of these children who are being abused and neglected. In keeping a job, you need to develop some critical and definite character traits that aid sustainability. One of those traits is patience. Even though I could stay there and learn to be patient, I just couldn't take what those children were facing.

In fact, I saw the effect it had on some of the workers who encountered the abuse or death of a child at the hands of their parents. The desire to help and just be there for them is not enough. It takes an anointed individual to be successful and effective for that. Yes! Only an anointed person can function there accurately. The word anointing simply means the divine ability bestowed upon someone to do what seems hard naturally. Even though anyone could be patient and learn patience, I understood that dispensing your energies on what you're not graced for is a mere waste of energy meant to do another work.

The Bible says in Act 10:38, *"How God anointed Jesus of Nazareth with the Holy Spirit and with power, who went about doing good and healing all who were oppressed by the devil, for God was with Him."* This verse reveals that whatever good Jesus did, it was because He was empowered to do so. The anointing He received enabled Him to step beyond all limitations and help others.

My fear of amounting to what they said led me to step into someone else's path for my life. I was trying to make myself do what society said I was "supposed" to do. Many students across colleges are trapped in the empty chase after a certificate or course that never matches up with their makeup fabrics. Oh! That's what's working now—so you must do this if you will be relevant and influential. We live in a society where you'll be judged on what you wear, what you do, your taste in a certain field, what you look like, and your behavior. But then, the ignorance of our uniqueness and individuality never makes us rise like a phoenix beyond societal influence.

I stayed in that tiny little box of ignorance for so long— conforming to the model of the world's systems and what it says about me. But things never worked out for me by subscribing to such standards. And funny enough, I was that student that would be so frustrated with the college curriculum. It never made sense to me! I mean, why should I need to take these "prerequisites" that had nothing to do with my major. Those were discouragers for me every time I would set myself up to pursue a college degree. I probably had about seven different start dates and still only walked out with a general associate's degree. The associate's degree only came about because I had felt I had given the nursing degree attempt my all.

However, it all ended when I received a B- in biology, but a B was required to proceed to clinical. That really hurt me. Part of the frustration was me having my agenda and no patience for something that was a waste of time and didn't make a difference either way. Before I proceed, can I tell you about the danger of impatience and having a plan different from God's plan from the life of Sarai? She had waited for several years for the promise of God to give her a child. But then, she advised Abram to make other plans without exercising patience. She said to Abram, *"See now, the LORD has restrained me from bearing children. Please, go into my maid; perhaps I shall obtain children by her." And Abram heeded the voice of Sarai."* Genesis 16:2

It looked like a perfect plan, right? Abram and Sarah had their agenda well planned and structured, but all they did was delay or postpone pre-ordained timing. Like me, Abram and Sarai took in Hagar—a slave, as their plan B, and they suffered unnecessary delay. Are you patient in your decision-making or impulsive? Understand that decisions are keys to transitions in our lives. We must make them patiently—not hastily.

Another part was that I wasn't disciplined enough to stay on task through the required classes to get to my major courses. From his wealth of wisdom, King Solomon says, *"The soul of a lazy man desires, and has nothing; But the soul of the diligent shall be made rich."* Proverbs 13:4. He added in chapter 18 verse 9 that *"whoever is slack in his work is a brother to him who destroy."* Think about these verses. Lack of discipline can turn your journey of one mile into an endless trip into blackness. This is why George Washington said, *"Discipline is the soul of an army. It makes small number formidable; procures success to the weak, and esteem to all."* No matter how weak you seem in the face of fulfilling your beautiful dreams and visions, if discipline becomes a permanent portrait on the walls of your interaction with purpose and destiny, you're a stone's throw to success. You see, because of my lack of discipline, the soldier within me quaked to the fearful thoughts that kept ravaging my mind.

I attempted online schooling, and that was an epic fail. I need a human being in front of me. And not just a human being, someone with a sense of humor and that can be relatable. I didn't like know-it-all teachers either. They would speak and respond to you as though you should know the material they are supposed to teach and educate you on already. Excuse me, Ms. Parker, I really don't want to ask you this question because I know you don't like them...

Part of what causes a storm of unrest and dissatisfaction each time we're about to cross into a new phase in life is the fear of the unknown. "Oh! What kind of job will fit me perfectly and settle my bills? Goodness! I need a spouse too." These are some of the thoughts that joggle our minds. The book of Philippians 4:6-7 says, *"Be anxious for nothing, but in everything by prayer and supplication, with thanksgiving, let your requests be made known to God; and the peace of God, which surpasses all understanding, will guard your hearts and minds through Christ Jesus.."* In the pursuit of your goals and dreams, always beware of anxiety and unnecessary fear. The Bible prescribed a solution here: Prayer and supplication. These two powerful spiritual principles are good enough to force everything into alignment. But when you allow fear and needless rambling considerations to overwhelm your mind, your eyes will become blind to the endless possibilities at your disposal.

For me, I feared that I would not be taken seriously or be considered at having a chance at starting a career with a great company wanting a bachelor's degree to do so. But I still decided to let go of college in 2017, take an Associates in General Studies, and pursue entrepreneurship while working full time. I have been labeled and looked upon as a leader my whole life by people who know me and don't know me. But it was I who couldn't see the leader in me because I felt untrained, uneducated, inadequate, and inferior to those leaders that I was inspired by. Not realizing it, my perception of myself was the reason I felt as though I had nothing else to offer this world. Sounds just like Peter and John in Acts 4:13-14. They were found to be uneducated and uneducated but had been in the presence of Jesus. Wouldn't you rather be untrained but in God's presence in rooms you may not qualify to be in according to the world? God can perform miracles in allowing others to see you as He sees you to get you to a place of authority, abundance, or in line with your destiny. God is your ultimate source for everything else; why not wisdom on another level? You have to align with how God sees and envisions you to elevate.

A correct perception of your complexity and importance is what guarantees your influence and the giant stride you will ever make. Lions move in the jungle with such audacity simply because they walk in the realities of their identity. When you lack a correct perception of your personality or individuality, you will be one of the Princes Solomon talked about in Ecclesiastes 10:7. He said, *"I have seen servants on horses, While princes walk on the ground like servants."*

Sincerely, many people with kingly destinies walk on foot because they lack the understanding and perception of who they are! No wonder God said His people are destroyed for lack of knowledge.

I had no clue about my contribution to this world. What was the purpose of my existence? How would I have the ability to educate, become an expert, or impact anyone if I am not educated? What wisdom or difference can I make on this earth before God calls me home? Or am I at this point because He is about to call me home? I can just imagine hearing God's deep, stern voice, "Angels go, get Ebony! I have no use for her on earth anymore; she's just mossing along and taking up space. She's simply confused and lost." There's got to be more to my life. The only thing I can do at this point is live out what I know so far and wait to see what comes next. I can continue as a wife, a mother, and just plain Ebony White.

First, it took time for me to realize what exactly I needed. I felt incomplete, unfinished, and useless. The feeling of being incomplete was me, not whole or broken. This fire was ignited by feeling unworthy of people's time and attention just because I felt that I was not equipped enough to do what God called me to do. My understanding of God's will for service was weak. I never realized that I needed to understand that He already qualified me when God calls me to do something. He called me to tell and use my story, and no one can be more of an expert on my story than me. This is the power of uniqueness! Nobody is created with the same prototype as another. You're unique and special. While there's a universal will of God for all His creation yet, He has fashioned a specific will and purpose for you. Have you found yours?

So, I came to understand that God can choose to teach us hard lessons of life through unpalatable experiences if our heart is bent on disobeying Him—not wanting to submit! That's why I couldn't finish school toward a bachelor's degree. He didn't want me to finish just yet or, if ever. That may force me to tell a different story from the one He wants me to tell now. The feeling of being unfinished was an accurate and confirming one. God isn't done with me yet! He has been waiting for me to align with His plan and not my own. My plan was nothing like His, so I needed to surrender to His will for me.

Feeling useless has ended a lot of lives to suicide. Those of us who want to help, benefit, and add value to others don't like to be helpless. And when we feel helpless, we quickly cover it up with a false boldness that veils our lack of confidence. Have you ever wondered why this is so? The simple reason is that we don't want to look weak in the face of what we felt we have the inner capacity to bring a lasting solution to. Something tells me I don't need a piece of paper to validate me. I'm built for this! When you think about Peter (a foremost disciple of Jesus), his zeal, passion, love, and desire never to appear weak to anyone made him usability before the all-knowing Christ.

Yes, I needed to be used by God, and to achieve that, you need to be connected to God. Just like Peter, I wasn't yet weaned from my inability to own up and surrender to the one who could help me. For three good years, Peter hid his fears beneath the surface of Jesus' presence there with them. He literary never opened the inner fears he has nursed until Jesus broke fantastic news that began the journey of dependence for Peter.

Peter seems to have good plans in his heart for Jesus. He never wanted Jesus to take that tiring and a blood-draining trip to the cross. So, he held on to his beautiful plan without surrendering it to God's will. For God to connect Peter to Himself and show him how helpless man can be, Jesus told him in the book of Luke 22:31, *"and the lord said, Simon, Simon! Indeed, Satan has asked for you, that he may sift you as wheat."* What happened here is shocking and breaking news that announced the intention of the enemy to capitalize on Peter's fears to stop him from being an Apostle of Pentecost.

When you see Peter around, you may think here is a bold and unbending follower of his master. But see how his fear was revealed after Jesus was arrested and how connection back to God—the source of all strength brought the best out of him.

When You Respond in Fear; Peter's Version

[Luke 22:54-62]

Having arrested Him, they led Him and brought Him into the high priest's house. But Peter followed at a distance. Now when they had kindled a fire in the midst of the courtyard and sat down together, Peter sat among them. And a certain servant girl, seeing him as he sat by the fire, looked intently at him and said, "This man was also with Him." But he denied Him, saying, "Woman, I do not know Him." And after a little while another saw him and said, "You also are of them." But Peter said, "Man, I am not!" Then after about an hour had passed, another confidently affirmed, saying, "Surely this fellow also was with Him, for he is a Galilean." But Peter said, "Man, I do not know what you are saying!" Immediately, while he was still speaking, the rooster* crowed. And the Lord turned and looked at Peter. Then Peter remembered the word of the

Lord, how He had said to him, "Before the rooster crows,* you will deny Me three times." So Peter went out and wept bitterly.

The last statement above shows how Peter got connected back to God—the place of surrendering!

You see, when you have a connection or a relationship with God, you receive a clearer vision and peace with who you are. Your purpose will be made known to you through your relationship with God. He will guide you and teach you what you need to know to fulfill your destiny. Can you believe that the same Peter who denied Jesus because of fear of a young lady still grew to a place of strength and fulfillment? His vision became clearer, and he made peace with God too. Think about Paul in the scriptures. He was busy running on an expired prototype of God's intentions without knowing that God has shifted the ground rule.

He fought the will of God until he had a Damascus encounter that made Him surrender his will, and he got connected to purpose. What was the result of that encounter? The result was a brighter and clearer vision of what God wants to do with his life. Truth is, purpose gets defined and clearer when you're connected to the right source—God!

When God was ready to guide Paul into fulfilling his destiny, He sent him to Joppa to meet a man called Simon. From there, Paul was led and guided into the template of his destiny. See what God said about Paul in Acts 9:16: *"For I will show him how many things he must suffer for My name's sake."* He later gave his testimony in Acts 26:19 that he wasn't disobedient to the heavenly vision he received on his Damascus experience. Connection with God is what births your realities! If you miss God in your pursuit in life, you have missed the foundation of all essence. When you stay connected to God, He will begin to lead you into the things you should do and not do.

For instance, He led me to invest in personal development courses, books to read, and trades to learn. It is all education. As wonderful as those disciplines are, He still taught me through the book of Proverbs 18:16 that your gift, not your education/degree, makes room for you and will bring you before great men. Your gifts are like master keys that unlock the high places of honor and prestige for you. It can define your boundary of influence.

Finally, I learned or went through some things that cannot be taught by an instructor or be bought. Life teaches you the best lessons and gives the best wins. Lessons are valuable losses that are worth cherishing and can't be bought or stolen. It may require you first to take an "L" (loss) that gave you hell, to assure you **EARNED** the knowledge you **LEARNED**! Following God's wisdom and knowledge is your contribution to your purpose, His will, and plan for your life.

Chapter 9

I WILL be truthful to You

(You shall not bear false witness against your neighbor)

My Queen,

The parting of your lips to reveal your teeth that shines brightness, the twinkle of your eyes, and the beautiful sounds that come from the depth of a lovely heart as yours is all it takes to make me commit myself to you only. Seeing your smile completes my day from start to finish. It makes me want to help you accomplish your goals and give you the comfortable life you deserve, and to have all the reasons to smile.

It makes me feel like becoming a genie in a bottle so you can have wishes and get them. I've been with you, my dear, and I know. I know you have been through a lot. I understand the situations you've gone through and how you've been looked down on. It's your demeanor that captured me in you, your vulnerability to trust me and come off as though you are the most confident woman. Your fears, weaknesses, and strengths are what I want to know about you, the good and the bad.

I want to write them down in the diary of my love for you and read them every morning when I wake up. *Depression,* and I know how you feel. You made mistakes, but you need to show them you can do better. You have to prove yourself to the world. That should be the easy part. Do you think you can be better too? You have so much value inside of you that you can't see. You've hidden it so deep within. You've dug a large hole inside and dumped these treasures you have in it.

I promise to give you the best of me, to hold a lasting impression in your mind. I want your heart to belong to me, just as mine is for you, and only you. I want you to always think of me and call on me. I want to be the one that sits at the throne of your heart. I want to help you all the way through. I am here to be there for you, unlike Mr. Promises above. No matter what life throws at us, I will always be there to catch you. I'll hold your hands firmly and lovingly, so you won't fall, even when you stumble. It is you and me against the world, Ebony.

I care about you dearly. How you feel, and your emotions are my priority. No one can tell you how you feel or downplay how you feel. You have the right to express your feeling; no one should make you trap them inside you. If you are angry, be angry. If you are moody, be moody. If you are afraid, be afraid. Just be honest about it and don't apologize for it. You are human,

169

just like everyone else. You have blood and flesh and a heart like all others. You may not feel good every day but allow how you feel to be released.

Don't compress them in that black hole container and keep it in your soul. Your emotions should determine your next move. And when you move, I move, just like that! It's both of us facing all the rest. I'm with you every single second that ticks. I got your back like none other. I can give you all the love you need. I am that one you need in your life to make it a smooth and happy one. You deserve to be loved. If Abe is not giving you enough confirmation that he deserves you, he's not ready for you. He should show that he was lucky to have met someone like you. In truth, he doesn't deserve you. He should appreciate this about you.

All marriages have tough times–it isn't all rose and no thorns– but he should be willing to always affirm that you're more deserving than him because not many women could take on the role you did from the jump. You've always taken the jump, but now, it's time for someone to jump for you, and it's me…

Love, Fear

The Truth Will Set You Free

Truth isn't an alien concept to the human species, but it's always been ignored from the start. Pretending that it isn't even there, we reach over the bowl of truth and dip our fingers into that of insincerity with self and others. We are quick to spit out lies instead of simply stating the truth. If we are truthful with ourselves, our lives could have a bigger impact on others. We could become a root of motivation for the branches and leaves of people out there. Our life could be like a source of a spring that always nourishes others and keep their bodies hydrated with hope and positivity.

But we like to deny the faults we have in ourselves. We turn blind eyes to those that are our weaknesses and shine our pupils in our exalting habits. You know, like living in a world of self-induced oblivion when you, deep down, know the reality is all up around you. We hold other people accountable for telling lies to us, but we do not hold ourselves accountable for the lies we tell ourselves out of fear. We like to fault others, point out those faults and flaws to them. We tell others how they've hurt us. But we don't admit the flaws we have. And that with that, we're hurting ourselves. We're making the journey of tomorrow strenuous than it should be.

Think about the cause of Adam's fall and how he excused himself from admitting his fault. From the question God asked Adam and his response, we could conclude that the seed of self-defense has suddenly taken a firm root in his heart. The bible says, *"Then the LORD God called to Adam and said to him, "Where are you?"* (Genesis 3:9). Please, note what God asked him. Where are you? Isn't that a simple question that demands a straight answer like—I'm here under a tree or something? But here what Adam said. *"So he said, "I heard Your voice in the garden, and I was afraid because I was naked; and I hid myself."* (Genesis 3:10).

Has Adam answered God's question there? No! He tried to veil his fault under the disguise of fear and dread. He said I was afraid! But God said, where are you? There's a divine placement that occasions God's expectations over our lives. God placed them in the Garden of sufficiency and no lack but with an expectation that he and his wife remain true to Him. You see, we always stumble into the valley of nakedness when we try to cover our faults and pass the blame on others.

God asked Adam another simple question in verse 11, *"And He said, "Who told you that you were naked? Have you eaten from*

172

the tree of which I commanded you that you should not eat?" Instead of taking responsibility for his sin and fault, guess what he said to God. He quickly shifted the blame on his wife and said, *"Then the man said, "The woman whom You gave to be with me, she gave me of the tree, and I ate."* [12] Remember that fear was a resultant effect of the fall of man. Adam was never created to be afraid of anything. He carried the ruling DNA! The fall produced in him a fearful and dishonest personality.

What Fear Is

Growing up, I lost self-confidence that put me deeper in the darkness of the valley. The phases in my life and what had happened in them made me a lower version of myself. It was hard to hold my head up. The buoyancy of my self-esteem was punctured, and I sank. I shrank. Fear was my greatest undoing. The moment I accepted it with open hands into my life, it came in with its baggage of other negativities. It was the greatest challenge I have ever encountered. It was the one challenge that gave birth to several others that influenced my life wrongly. Fear was just like a big balloon filled with pus. As soon as I gave it the top space in my heart, the pregnancy, it had burst open and sprayed me with its slimy contents.

173

Fear might differ in meaning to various people due to their past experiences with it. It's been what everyone has encountered at some moment in their life. Even though the situations fear brought about were different, it is still that popular and infamous emotions-sucking insect we've come to know it as. I had searched it out and seen that fear was an acronym for a meaning larger than the four letters it displays. It was broader than it seemed. I saw that those four words were just like drumrolls for something bigger. The meaning for the acronym FEAR was stated as;

F-False

E-Evidence

A-Appearing

R-Real

Let's quickly unpack this life-sucking word and see it for what it is. First, the letter F, which stands for false, reveals the first internal reality of what fear contains. Fear is like a lonely world of falsehood, an ocean that seems deeper than its reality.

Even though that acronym seems okay, I wasn't going to accept the representation for the letter **E**. I could have gone with those meanings, but the word "evidence" didn't sit right with me. When I hear the word "evidence," the meanings I get in my head are "proof" or "facts." Evidence on its own is closely related to truth and really distant from the word *false* or *fake*. False facts sound contradictory in themselves. Saying something like the false proof is oxymoronic. It's not a fact if it's not true, and you have no proof if it is false. I searched my mind, knowing for sure that there has to be another word starting with the letter "E" that'll retake more with the other given meanings. As soon as I put my hand on my head to think, ding! I got it; it's EMOTIONS!

F-False

E-Emotions

A-Appearing

R-Real

Fear and Emotions

Emotions can be snakes in green grasses. They hide behind the facade of mere feelings when it's actually fear sponsoring them. When we tell ourselves lies, it's out of fear. We don't want to admit the truth because we aren't sure if we'd be able to face it. We can't bear to live with reality, so we pretend to ourselves. The great writer and poet, Ralph Waldo Emerson once said, *'When a resolute young fellow steps up to the great bully, the world, and takes him boldly by the beard, he is often surprised to find it comes off in his hand, and that it was tied on to scare away the timid adventurer.'*

Since we can't embrace the truth with a heart of boldness like that young fellow, we accept it's better to fold it all up into a big, fat package and dump it in a trashcan somewhere in the corner of our minds. We don't want to experience the shock that comes from telling the truth, especially to ourselves. Telling lies to ourselves, it's all from emotions. We satisfy ourselves with the justifications we think we have when something doesn't go according to plan.

These emotions spring up inside of us, and we push them to the forefront of our outlook. We leave them in the room of our hearts to determine how to react to situations. Just like that famous saying, 'You are in your feelings.' Put that saying in any situation where you were putting yourself down about a failed attempt, mistake, or even if things just didn't go as planned; it is saying, You are afraid of something happening, fear!

Fear has a lot to do with self-confidence. When you allow it in and make no attempt to overcome it, it takes you as weak. When fear senses you've surrendered to it, it mars your being, starting from your confidence. When your confidence and esteem are down, it becomes easy to let in other kinds of negativity. You wouldn't be able to repel them because you'd think you aren't able to fight it off.

See, fear makes you give excuses for yourself; it makes you stay right down when you can as well rise to your feet. Fear lets your emotions influence your decisions, it appears to you as help out of a difficult situation, but later on, you realize it was actually eating into your emotional health. I learned these the hard way through life experiences. Fear makes you say something like, "I am not qualified/ trained to do this!" The point here is that it isn't really that you aren't qualified for it; it's that you don't want to admit failure to yourself, so you give excuses for it when it comes.

I've told myself this lie in fear of failing or getting embarrassed or being rejected. I didn't even want to try anything out if I wasn't a hundred percent sure of my success in it. The fear failure injects! So, I let myself believe I couldn't do it because probably it wasn't my area of expertise or so. I didn't admit the fear I had, didn't tell myself that truth. Talk of lying to yourself and not admitting your weakness. It is easier to accept disappointment if you already had negative feelings about it. That's how negativity builds within a person, creating "Negative Nancy or Nick." They create some sort of cover for themselves from that excuse. That lie, they use it as a shield to prevent getting hurt or feeling rejected.

A Lifeguard for A Drowning Soul

There is hope even when you're drowning. Not just drowning without screaming out for help! Imagine what happened to Peter in the book of Matthew 14:25-31 when fear took hold of him.

"Now in the fourth watch of the night Jesus went to them, walking on the sea. 26 And when the disciples saw Him walking on the sea, they were troubled, saying, "It is a ghost!" And they cried out for fear. But immediately Jesus spoke to them, saying, "Be of good cheer! It is I; do not be afraid." And Peter answered Him and said, "Lord, if it is You, command me to come to You on the water." So He said, "Come." And when Peter had come down out of the boat, he walked on the water to go to Jesus. 30 But when he saw that the wind was boisterous, he was afraid; and beginning to sink he cried out, saying, "Lord, save me!" And immediately Jesus stretched out His hand and caught him, and said to him, "O you of little faith, why did you doubt?"

You see, Peter didn't sink because Jesus wasn't there. He sank because he was afraid. The moment fears gripped his heart; it held him like a helpless stone finding its way to the depths of the sea. Peter wouldn't drown helplessly when Hope Himself (Jesus) was right there. Peter never lost hope to the storm! He cried out for help. You see, sometimes we have help close to us as the hair on our body, but we are blind to them. And sometimes, we feel too proud to open up our wounds to people around us for a lasting cure.

When I was at one of the lowest points in my life, I realized that it was a turbulent time for me, and my business advisor introduced me to a colleague of his who is a life coach. Immediately I knew that he had what I wanted at that moment of my life; I needed his services. So, I let him in on everything about my life. I still remember that as the best investment and decision I had made in a long time. It was the best gift I'd paid for myself and my husband. It helped my self-esteem rise to the surface and taught me lessons I wouldn't have dreamt of learning in a thousand years.

The life coach stated things he saw in my husband and me that I couldn't see happening for a long shot. Even though that wasn't the first time I had heard it, I wasn't farsighted enough to really check it out. He opened my eyes to the fact that, first, I have a story to tell and that someone needs to hear it. What has been happening in my life, all of them, are for the benefit of someone out there that's probably passing through the same phases as I have. I had to write it down and communicate it to them. The pieces of our broken self are there to help others build a more effective life and bring the light of wisdom on their darkened path.

Secondly, God wants me to share my story to motivate and inspire all walks of people as a step toward my destiny. It was like His mission for me; I had to use my life as a ladder to help people up when they're sinking. My story, the challenges, the lessons were to help others up and fulfill His plan. And thirdly, he said if God has destined for me to do this, He has already qualified and trained me to do so. He'd already given me the education and tools I needed to share my life story. He'd given me the muse already.

My training was Life. Life itself was my workout routine, as God is my personal trainer. The experiences and phases I'd gone through were the exercises I had to endure to build backing and strength for this chapter of my life. Being a teen mother was some weight that I thought I couldn't bear. I thought I wouldn't be able to get past it all, but I did. There were many other situations I hadn't been sure of overcoming, which I thankfully did. Unhealthy relationships, negativity, hopelessness, foul emotions and thoughts, and friendships were the calories and fat I needed to burn off.

Everyone is not meant to be in every season in your life. Your life is like a book of many stories. Not every character should be in every chapter of the story. The word of God needed to become my new diet, nourishment. I needed to take it morning, noon, and evening. It had to be the appetizer, main meal, and dessert for me. Prayer was to be the vitamins that supplemented the nutrients I took in. This meal plan showed me all the nutrients I needed to have and sustain. And the waste I needed to get rid of. The more "my trainer" went over my "meal plan", the easier it became to understand and stick to it. I found out that I needed it to get me through the day and help me breathe better in polluted areas of life that I was exiting.

Realizing how bad it becomes when I refuse to stick to this healthy meal plan and decide to eat junk, I made it an everyday thing. The treadmill is the path from the decisions we make to keep me moving. No matter how fast or slow I'm going or what path I'm walking or running on, I have my "personal trainer" covering, encouraging, and overseeing what I do to help me stay on and keep me going. He has also given me the strength not to fall off or get tired of the constant movements. I also can get off to sightsee. The judgment and not-so-beautiful situations I went through were the muscle aches. They were the constant pains I had to deal with. The harder I worked, the more it occurred. I continued moving, so the aches were constant. But the more it kept coming about, the easier it was for me to endure it. My tolerance began to build up against the aches, pains, and ability to just give up. What did that quote say? "The more mountains you finish climbing, the more that comes your way, and the stronger you become." It was just like starting an exercise: it might seem kind of hard and tough the first three times. But, as you go through it, you know the ropes. It isn't all that hard as the first times anymore. That was how it was for me. I was placed in situations in which I have to rise against, revive from, and release many times.

So yes, I was trained for this! The saying "I am not good enough" was used when things didn't go according to my plan. That was when I wouldn't admit my fear to myself and lead myself out of it. When fear was eating deep inside my guts, and I didn't have the boldness to shake it off.

Rise, Revive, Release

Currently, I am also a licensed realtor. I remember that the test to get my license was not that easy for me. I found interest in real estate by watching the fix and flip TV shows and attending seminars. I wanted to pursue that career. I couldn't decide if I wanted to be licensed, but what was it going to hurt. I decided I wasn't going to lose anything if I got the license, so I went ahead.

I took the class and needed to prepare for the exam. I did what I thought I needed to do to pass. I prepared well for the exam, but I realized that was not good enough because I failed it by 12 points.

By the time I had taken the class, I was all in and had a plan set out before me. I wanted it so bad, and I failed. The testing site was about an hour's drive away from my home. From the time I pulled off from there until I got off the highway, I'd put so much junk in my head that it pushed me further down into a sinking hole that I had been looking forward to it and had failed incited inside me a sinking feeling of disappointment. My spirit went low. I feared that I was wasting more time and was a bit embarrassed.

Finally, I found something that could be beneficial in many ways outside of going to college. Right then, I gave up on that career. I pursued other causes that would add an advantage to my family and me. But I realized that I still had a desire to do it even after almost a year. I wanted to reapply so badly that I consulted with my husband about the fact that I may not pass and could waste a lot of money. Again, I had him considered all that was at stake and if I could still risk going back to the college for the license test. He encouraged me to go ahead; I had his full support.

The material had changed from when I initially took it. Once again, I went for the classes and retook the exam. When the result was released, I was only five points away from passing that time. I narrowly failed again. The fact that the number I missed passing was less than the first time was enough gas to get me to the third attempt. I believed if I sat for the test again, I'd definitely pass.

One week later, I took the test again. Guess what, I PASSED! It was such a happy moment for me. I was so excited I'd finally got what I'd been seeking. The two failed attempts to get the license taught me down lessons that helped shape my life for the better. It taught me tenacity, determination, and that God can use it all. I recently discovered that God's ultimate goal for me was to be a real estate investor and not a realtor. That's the side that I am meant for, but that step was used in the process to show me things I may need later to understand. There are people I am to help that's looking for honest realtors to assist or advise them through the purchasing or selling process. I have told myself many times that "This will never work." I recognized that as still fear of being disappointed. I didn't want to get my hopes high and have them eventually deflated. So, I just expect the possibility of failure before anything even happens. I'd fed myself all that junk of negativity and doubt before I realized I didn't always have the fight I needed to prove that side of me wrong because life was still training me.

The job that I previously talked about that initialized my career with The State, I thought that I would never hear from anyone about that job. I'd forgotten all about it. But, when they called, they responded to me quicker than any other job during my search. I also had issues accepting blessings right in front of me because I was still punishing myself and listening to naysayers too. I felt I didn't deserve them, and this way, I lost a lot of favor I could've enjoyed. And I was still listening to the naysayers too. I took in all they served me. This would later account for or be a part of increasing my low self-confidence.

When I would just sit back and think about how caring, loving, supportive, and protective my husband is to our family and me, it was unreal to me. I felt like Cinderella. It was all like the Alice in wonderland story. The uneducated teen mom who had been pulled down and no one expected anything from her life, now getting a fantastic guy to love and care. It was a blessing and sweet grace. I always thought, "I don't deserve him!" Hell, I was still learning myself and how to love. He was willing to learn me with me regardless of how frustrating it could be. He was so supportive he walked the journey with me, right by my side, with my hands in his.

185

Even with all the stress my life seemed to come with, he was always right there. During the moments I needed him, he was always there. With a listening ear to take in all I say, a ready shoulder prepared to take my face when it's soaked and soothing lips that comfort the troubled seas of my soul. Lord, where did he come from?! He always seemed like an angel sent to me but in human form. Abe came at a time in my life when I wasn't even looking for love or just a man, for that fact. I was set on the future and did not need the love saga then. But Abe showed me how he needed me, with me being my messed-up self. It was so amazing to see he was able to stay right there with me, uncomplaining, even when I wore him out. Sometimes, I would push him away because I felt he could be with someone better. I felt I didn't deserve a man so loving and understanding like him. He is a good man, valuable, and priceless. The truth all boiled down to Abe knowing his worth; I just needed to discover my worth to be set free!

Chapter 10

I WILL be generous to You
(You shall not covet)

My Ebony,

I have been looking out for you since you came to me. My eyes have been fixed intensely but lovingly on you. I have watched you grow up into this blooming rose. You've developed from that cute little girl into an even more beautiful woman. I've been there all the time. I've always watched you. I was there, waiting, on the day your tiny cry pierced the gloominess of this world. I was there while you crawled, babbled, and stood. I wasn't absent when you started learning. And as you grow, I find myself sticking more to you.

In your happy mood, I had smiled and laughed with you. In your low moments, I've wiped the tears off your full, red cheeks even as I restrained my tears from escaping my red eyes. In the times you thought you were alone, those times you felt lonely, I was there by your side. Every morning when you wake, and when you sleep at night, I've been there. I've seen you through it all, darling. You grew up alone because it was meant for you to learn how to be alone. You were destined to run the race of life on your own, darling. You had to go through it all by yourself. But I have spared myself for you. I have decided, and I'm determined to run this race with you. I have made the promise to myself, and now to you, that I will be the love you can ever have. I can be a rug so you wouldn't have to walk on the cold, rough field of life. I can be the masseuse that helps you relax after the cruel heat life emits.

Resentment *teaches* us how to look at this world as cold, protects us, and I want to be your warmth. This world is cruel, and I want to be your happiness. This world is sad, and I want to be responsible for your laughter. This world is empty, and I want to fill it up with only me and you. I want to be your green when the world is all dry. I want to be the color that lights up this drab world. I want to be the reason you're happy. Everything that "God" has allowed this earth to be, I want to be the opposite for you. I want to be the opposite of the pain, hurt, ache, and tears He's always given.

He says He made this world beautiful and bright, but there's gloom, hate, and sadness, and so much ugliness all around. What kind of god just sits around and allows His creations to suffer or be ridiculed, disappointed, or broken-hearted? And He watches them go through all these, untouched! It's unbelievable how He sees everything, does nothing, and still makes futile promises, isn't it? He just hangs around, eyes intense, watching as everything unrolls. He only sees; He never does anything to change ill situations. He wants you to learn from being rejected, so He allows you to be denied or just not qualified for something you may need or want that isn't a bad thing. Even though He says He has the power to change your bad situation to an amazingly perfect one, He has never done so. Because He has lessons to teach you, He takes you through the kind of horror that could tear your spirit apart. He lets you lack, and when you ask, He doesn't answer. He has the "power" to make things work in your favor and doesn't use it, just watches.

Now, what kind of power is that? Which god does that kind of evil? My love, I will climb mountains, walk over the fire, fight like Hercules, travel across the violent seas, and even go to outer space to bring you back a star to show you how much you shine in my eyes. You are worth more than the entire universe put together. You shine more than the sun, moon, and stars in one big bulb. So, it sickens me to see you hurt and in pain. My heart knows no peace when yours is troubled. I live for you; I'm here for you. I'm all yours.

You know, that's why we shut down from everything to show God He isn't all that mighty as He says. His words are only lather of soap floating away minutes after He says them. Even the cry of that in fire moves Him not. I have seen you pray and talk to this whisperer of a man. I've heard you weep in the presence of Him whom you call God. You've cried out your hurts, pains, and frustrations at His unmoving feet. You've written Him letters in your heart, letters that tell of your emptiness and desires. You were pouring your heart out for something that He will turn around and give to someone else. What a tease that is for someone that has true desires for things she needs?

That person will be the main person to rub it in your face with, 'If He can do it for me, and He can do it for you!' What a joke! They both play games of betrayal and condescension. How do you know I haven't already asked for that? I have probably been asking for it longer or before you even came to it. I'm sorry if I can see how special you are, but others can't. For some reason, He must not see you "worthy" of the thing you have already asked for. He doesn't deem you good enough for what you asked. But, I tell you, your worth is far more valuable than all these other children of His. You are far more beautiful, more graceful, and full of worth than anyone of them. You are good and pure for me and to me.

I see no fault in you. As my eyes behold you, they behold marvelous perfection. I see beautiful worlds in your eyes. They are entrances to colorful realms. Your fingers are graceful. Your lips are goodness. Your cheeks bloom the red of rises. And your feet, they are as swift and enchanting as the antelope. There is nothing that can change what I see when I look at you amongst others. To me, you are special, different, and unique. You've been and will always be like that to me. You certainly deserve all that you ask and more. You are worth more than anyone else is. You are priceless.

Love, Fear

Growing Up

As a child, I grew up on the "Flipside" of the city of Saginaw, Michigan, with both of my parents in the household along with my two older siblings. I had a happy and stress-free childhood. Both of my parents had good-paying careers, so we lived just fine. My sister and I are thirteen years apart, and my brother and I are fifteen years apart. Because of the huge age difference between my siblings and me, I grew up pretty much as an only child, even though they would take me places with them and let me hang out with them.

One childhood advantage to having such grown-up siblings is that I rarely heard the answer "no" from them. I was hardly refused any request I laid before them. I was given almost everything I asked from them. And as far as my parents were concerned, I only heard no when I asked to have company right after church or stayed outside past curfew. Other than that, I was free and had all I needed at the tip of my pretty fingers. My entire family adored me. I was the baby of the family. I didn't have to work hard to get anything because I had most time what I needed or wanted, or it wasn't far out of my reach.

I wasn't high maintenance either, wanting expensive clothes and things. I was given some expensive things but didn't have to ask for them. I was satisfied with life; I had nothing to worry about. With these, I might have as well been a princess: all I needed was a palace and some maids to attend to me. Later in life, I saw that my king of upbringing was a blessing and a curse at different times in my life. Not getting no from my parents or siblings during childhood played out its disadvantage later.

Don't get it twisted; I appreciate my parents for making sure we didn't struggle. They provided my needs and even my wants, and for that, I am thankful. They were doing what was expected of good parents. That's why I pushed to make sure my oldest biological daughter had what she needed. If I needed to swallow my pride and stay home with my parents longer until I could afford my place comfortably, then that's what had to be done. Just like them, I'd do anything to make sure my daughter had a good life. The only thing about my childhood that still affects me is, I was never challenged or pushed to the limit. There was no longing or thirst inside me to gear me up. Where there's no lack, there can't be any yearning. Where there's abundance, hunger isn't a thing. I saw what the world really is when I left home and my parents and started life independently. Because I always had everything growing up, I wasn't easily adjusted to the new world I began to see. I could have as well been conservative if it were possible, but life has to happen. I didn't have what it takes to be determined to do something until the very end. Likewise, I was clueless about what it takes to learn endurance, perseverance, tenacity, drive, fight, and hard work. These core values were out of the curriculum in my upbringing. That was what happened to me.

Growing Up: Dealing with Rejection

Even before you say it, I am still learning, and I'm still a work in progress. Still, I know I still have a lot to learn about life on the journey of self-discovery. And I still have my quota to contribute to this world. I know I'm still going through the processes that will help me emerge as a better version of myself. But self-awareness is half the battle. It wasn't all about me not fully knowing myself yet. I've been facing greater challenges because of the opportunity I had as a child to get answers to almost all my requests.

One of them was rejection. Rejection, for someone with a childhood like mine, isn't easy to deal with. Being pampered all your life and then suddenly, everything changes– it's difficult to accept that kind of change. When I was told things like, No, not at this time, maybe later, not yet try again sometime or anything that did not insinuate a firm "yes," it was heartbreaking. Being something new to me, always crushed me. That heartbreak would come from what I saw as rejection that resulted in quitting and starting something else.

I start, rethink, and then quit. I would get all interested initially, and on the journey, I might feel it was too much for me to go through, and I'd eventually stop and start another journey. I always felt rejected somewhere along the way by even the slightest challenge. I'd think I couldn't get through it all, so I'd turn my back to it. I had an interest that I'd love to pursue; I would and then lose the will to continue halfway.

For example, when I would jump from one major to another in college, that was heartbreak when I was rejected with the feeling that it wasn't going to be worth the time spent studying or the debt that I'd accrue. If it seemed to require more than what I found necessary, I didn't complete it. That was my problem in completing my degree. I would start and then stop. I didn't think I was good enough to do it.

I experienced a lot of rejections in those years, from others and even from myself. I rejected chances that would have done me a lot of good, just because I didn't think I could keep up with them. I didn't undertake projects I was supposed to because I thought I might fail. The fear of disappointment was always there. I was always afraid of the unknown, "What if it didn't go as it should? What if I just make fun of myself? What if I get myself embarrassed and ridiculed?" So many what-ifs always show up. And the opportunities I did sign in for, I wasn't able to find the will to go through with.

Denial and Jealousy

Through personal experience, I got to know that being refused something and getting bitter goes hand in hand with those who allow their emotions to lead them. As I'd written earlier, I had the habit of beginning and walking out halfway. No matter how calm it was, crossing every river always got me going back to the shore. After, I'd deny myself of what could have been if I pressed on. I'd always be hurt seeing someone else succeed at what I had been pursuing and chose to quit. It used to be very painful to see someone succeed where I really wanted to but failed.

I felt bad about myself for not being able to get through it all as the others did. And seeing those who'd succeeded, I'd imagine myself taking their place of achievement. This made a negative emotion of envy rise inside of me. I would then become jealous and bitter, though not to the point I would hate on people, but I wondered why I couldn't have done the same thing, why I couldn't push on to the end like others. I was always like, God, why couldn't you bless me with the determination to do the same thing? What is it about me that I am not capable of the very same thing? Is it me not wanting it enough, or is it my attitude behind it when someone reaches the top of the mountain I am trying to climb?

I would try to force-feed my self-happiness for the next person, tried to look happy that they made it, but that was exhausting and short-lived. Such pretense was so stressful for me I couldn't keep on with it for too long. I didn't realize that when you don't give accolades, encourage people, and bless them sincerely; it blocks your blessing. I wanted what they now have instead of wanting God to help me get it done as well. I coveted the results of these people's sweat and hard work. I never wished that I could be given the strength to go through all they gave to achieve success.

Likewise, I didn't trust that if He did it for them, He could do it for me too. I realize now that if I'd tapped into that grace that helped others succeed, I wouldn't have been repeating that same cycle for as long as I did. If I'd gotten that solid faith in my heart about the possibilities in God, I'd have gotten what I wanted a long time before. I didn't believe in Him and the endless possibilities that come with trusting in His power completely. My lack of faith and hope in Him further built a cave of impossibilities that I had to live in. I took challenges as proof that I wasn't made for a particular pursuit. Mere hurdles I should cross, not even failure this time, got me turning back to the beginning. I didn't think I could jump over them and continue the run. I started to see roadblocks as "no" that built up to the fear of rejection, not the acceptance to be motivated to get a "yes."

In My Feelings

Here are a few of the negative emotions I allowed to be poured into my life attempting to keep me from the woman I am called to be. What they did and how they affected me. These emotions summarize what I went through in the spanking palms of rejection.

1   Bitterness

Bitterness was one of the foul and corrupting medicines I had injected inside of me. This bitterness came with jealousy. The success of others, especially in areas where I'd have loved to succeed, made me bitter. I got so jealous it became hard for me to even send them a congratulatory message with the whole of my heart. I had to keep suppressing the bitterness, as long as it took to give a fake smile and prevent it from getting obvious on my face. I began to ask the question why. Why did it have to be me still trying? Why can't I succeed as well? Why can I not have that determination in me, even if it's just a streak of it? Why could I not have the smile of the victory plastered on my face as well? These why questions also made me begin to doubt God. I didn't want to accept that He could help me out. I lost faith. And hope. I had thrown my belief in Him away. The fact that I had no faith in God made me not get what I wanted. I guess it was to teach me the lesson that God lives, and He answers prayers that are rich in faith and trust in who He is.

So, you see, bitterness started a chain of other negative influences. Bitterness resulted in jealousy, which in turn altered my identity and made me a person of pretense. Pretense caused me to question God, which meant I had lost my faith in Him. And my lack of faith made me stagnant.

2.   Self-doubt

My years away from my home and parents witnessed a downpour of damage to my self-belief. The teenage pregnancy I had, and all were incidents that really tested the value I thought I had. My self-worth was bought on a platter of uncertainties. I began to have little faith in myself; I didn't want to believe I could do anything huge. I underestimated myself, and it bounced back on me.

I was afraid of being disappointed. Disappointment has its sickening way of lowering our self-will and self-pride. I had a fear of the unknown. You never can know what will happen the next day, so I made sure to always keep my hopes down, so I won't be rejected and have my bubbles of pride burst. I couldn't face embarrassment, too, even if I don't know if it's going to happen. When I did experience it, it was a great killjoy for me. These fears made me hide from the spotlight and even lessen the value I have for myself.

I believed I could do nothing, and as written, I have false excuses to hide my fears. Doubting the wonders, I could perform catapulted me into the space of less confidence in myself. The more I believed I couldn't do something, the more I said the words, "I can't do this," to myself, and the more my confidence shrank. As my boldness decreased, so did my identity. That lady with low self-confidence wasn't who I was meant to be, as I later realized in God. I simply lost myself in the world of negativity.

3   Lack of Will

This might have been a result of the satisfying childhood I had, but I let it consume me. That's saying that goes, "Where there is a will, there is a way," isn't incorrect. Yes, I wasn't satisfied with where I was all those years, watching others live up to the dreams I had. I wasn't happy to watch while others had achievements. And I lamented about this.

But, you know, when all you do is whine and whine without taking any step towards working things out, you will remain in the same spot even years after. I didn't have the will and determination. I couldn't make decisions and stick to them. And underestimating the only one who could have helped me worsened it all. As they say, old habits die hard. Lack of will wasn't exactly a habit for me, but it was a phenomenon, a seed my years as a kid grew and nurtured. That seed has grown so big inside me that I couldn't manage or control it. I had to ask for help from one that wouldn't only cut it off from the stem but also uproot all traces of the roots– God. This was where I made a mistake; I invited my lack of will to sabotage the entrance and help of that One.

4   Fear

And this is the biggest one of them all, fear. Fear was the cause for everything. For all other destructive touches, I had in me then, fear was the initiator. And what sprouted this fear? The times of shifting, change, or maybe the resistance to change is where the fears snuck in at. You know, I was getting all comfy in the life I lived with my parents and siblings that I didn't suppose it would stop. I might have thought that was how it was meant to be forever. And when I saw how the world is, how uncomfortable it can get sometimes, it was hard to adjust to the change.

I couldn't bear all the problems that the wind of change brought, so I drilled a tiny hole for an external that could help me through that challenging period of my life. Fear came in through the outlet, sat as the ruling force of my being, and began to direct. It made that tiny space wider, so other foreigners like itself can gain access to my life. Fear was it that set the pace for most of the difficult situations I encountered. But I stand here in bold pursuit to be generous with accolades for others who are pursuing dreams and overcoming things under the uniqueness of their calling and purpose.

Chapter 11

Love,

Me

My Love Letter to Fear

He who gets wisdom loves his own soul; He who keeps understanding will find good.

Proverbs 19:8 (NKJV)

In all these instances, we allow fear to take over, dictate our reactions, how we viewed ourselves, and manipulate us, resulting in the negativity we made our reality. Our ultimate mistake is allowing fear to take God's place in our lives, being obedient to our fears instead of God's demands & promises. These letters are from the things that were keeping me from my purpose. Truth is that every believer will face the challenge of overcoming obstacles to their purpose. The biggest limitation to my purpose was my sluggish obedience.

You see, God required certain things from me, and it took me a long time to respond or follow through. Those things were simple demands from God. Your purpose will find you when your environment is not so crowded. Is your life too busy to receive God's ideas? Does the noise of the world surround you filling your ear with every piece of information except God? Does it drown out God's voice, robbing you of His priceless guidance? God loves to speak to us when our heart is at rest and our minds are focused on Him. Many people miss out on their purpose because they are always preoccupied with the wrong things. Indeed, we're too wrapped up in life, not allowing Him to set us apart toward our destiny.

God loves it when we take some time off to reflect on our lives and be with Him. Such moments create room for strategic thinking. Strategic thinking gifts us with the ability to see not just our side but the enemy's side as well. Having the culture of reflecting on your life is biblical and will help you live circumspectly as a believer. You see bits and pieces of God-aided strategic thinking in the scriptures. For example, Psalm 90:12 says, *"So teach us to number our days, That we may gain a heart of wisdom."* This scripture is about being sensitive and wise in the way you use your time. It shows you that you're required to give an account for your life.

How purpose-driven are you? Are your days unproductive, or do they bear fruits? Is God being glorified by your life and activities? Whose voice are you listening to? What are your limitations, and how can you eliminate them? Where do you want to be? All these are questions that strategic thinking provides answers to. It helps you to meticulously inspect areas of your life you might have ignored.

When something is visible, it creates logic or understanding of how it operates. This systematic thinking is what can guide us through obstacles. Our endurance becomes stronger and built to withstand the power God wants to equip you with, His strength. In my efforts, I am led to bring awareness of how fear is used to deceive our inner man.

While Jesus was on earth, He performed many miracles. But one of Jesus' most spectacular miracles is the act of walking on water. The day Jesus walked on water, Peter asked to join him, and within minutes, he too was walking on water towards Jesus. But Peter's supernatural experience was short-lived. Why, because He allowed fear to invade his heart.

Although Peter walked on water as though it were solid ground, he was frightened by the waves. They were scary enough when he was in the boat. However, because he was closer to the water, his fear increased. He forgot that it was by Jesus' power that he stood on water. So immediately he allowed fear, he began to sink.

Just as fear came into Peter's heart and stopped him from experiencing God's tremendous power, fear comes into our hearts to steal our testimonies. It comes to sink our faith and drown our commitment to God in the cares of this world.

The same way Peter lied about the power of the waves to drown him, the enemy feeds us with False Emotions Appearing Real so that we can unintentionally disobey these demands from God. Ecclesiastes 12:13 says, *"Let us hear the conclusion of the whole matter: Fear God and keep His commandments, For this is man's all."* Your obedience to God is more important than anything because it's obedience that qualifies us for God's blessings. Check out these two texts:

1. *"If you are willing and obedient, You shall eat the good of the land;"* Isaiah 1:19

2. *"If they obey and serve Him, They shall spend their days in prosperity, And their years in pleasures.* Job 36:11

You know, the Bible reveals that we're in spiritual warfare with the enemy. Therefore, just as physical battles are fought with strategy, we must use God-given strategy to overcome the enemy's strategy.

Dear Fear,

We have had quite some time to get to know each other. You have learned a few things about me, and I have learned a few things about you too! I found that exposure to something unknown eliminates excuses of the known. I have reflected on situations in my life where I allowed you in. Those were days of ignorance. Now I see why the Bible says in Hosea 4:6, *"My people are destroyed for lack of knowledge. Because you have rejected knowledge, I also will reject you from being priest for Me; Because you have forgotten the law of your God, I also will forget your children."* Not knowing the great damage you can cause, I gave you access to my heart, thoughts, and actions. But this can no longer happen! I have been placed in a position where the purposes of those situations were made clear and concise. Yes, now I can say and speak boldly like Job, *"But He knows the way that I take; When He has tested me, I shall come forth as gold.* (Job 23:10). Everything I experience was for my beautification. Surely, gold will remain unrefined and undesirable until it has gone through fire. My trial seasons felt like they would destroy me, but I am becoming who God wanted me to be.

In God's sight, the time we spent in the fire of refining is not lost time. Consider Abram and Sarai. They spent a long time waiting for the fulfillment of God's promise. At several intervals, they were frustrated and almost gave up. Out of frustration, they made mistakes and made decisions without God. They were hasty because they didn't know God's priority. God isn't only interested in giving us gifts and making us great. Much more, God wants us to become the people He wants us to be, in character and nature.

All those years Abram and Sarai spent holding on to God, it shaped them into the people who were qualified for God's blessings. Before then, they couldn't host the kind of blessings God wanted to release. Their names changed when their capacity changed to Abraham and Sarah. So while I was frustrated and angry against God, He was working on me inside out.

Conviction gave way to conquer and see the nice, green, grassy hill for what it really was. It was a bumpy, rocky, icy mountain that only gave way to allow me to get so far and then slip back to where I started. I saw that slipping off that mountain repeatedly was you trying to captivate me sometimes, and I don't like to be confined or backed into a corner.

I needed to see the ugly before the beauty. It's like that scripture in the book of Psalms that says, *"Search me, O God, and know my heart; Try me, and know my anxieties; And see if there is any wicked way in me, And lead me in the way everlasting."* (Psalm 139:23-24) God had to expose the contents of my heart so that I could repent and have a better relationship with Him. I had to take inventory and figure out what was crippling me. My handicap was my lack of fight. It is just as much of a handicap to have, as it is not to have. God seen that I needed a situation or circumstance that would build up my fight, determination, and tenacity that's in me. I had to become aware of the battle I was involved in and become a soldier who fought the good fight of faith. I didn't know that if I had Christ in me, I had what it takes to survive and overcome any storm life brings my way. Yes, God let me go through the fire to toughen me up.

I came from a two-parent household, a decent lifestyle, and not lacking anything. So, He chose to bless me with my first daughter as a teenager. He knew that it would take me some time to put you out and let Him in, which is why He started early. That's when I was introduced to **Mercy**. She hung with me for as long as she physically could until it became evident that I took her for granted. She was still there, but it just was in another form.

Again, I needed to experience the ugly before the beauty of things. There were times I wanted to give in or give up on the worst things, but because I knew I had my daughter relying on me, I couldn't. Sometimes God makes us strong by giving us a reason to fight. I wonder if I would have been persistent if I was alone. How could I quit when my baby girl needed me? She was my fight; she was my "why." Little children aren't aware of the limitations of their parents. They see their parents as their superheroes. I just couldn't let my daughter down. I saw days come and go where I did not want to be alive, but I thought of her first.

In all, she's one of the reasons I'm still here today. The areas I was more mature in were built up because of what she and I have endured. Romans 5:3-4 put it perfectly: *"And not only that, but we also glory in tribulations, knowing that tribulation produces perseverance; 4 and perseverance, character; and character, hope."* My sufferings taught me endurance even in the most challenging situations. My daughter stopped my heart from going cold; she kept it warm deep down inside. She helped me stay on my feet long enough to meet my husband and then passed the torch to him. Once I mastered a way to overcome the ugly, the beauty was my bird to soar.

I thought that you were protecting me from embarrassment, hurt, depression, worry, and insecurities. Instead, you were the hand, feeding those things within me, growing them, and nurturing them over me. You are indeed subtle, a manipulator, and a deceiver. Just as the serpent came to Eve as a friend, you came in the façade of someone who cared. I believed your calculated and manipulative words. Ultimately, I allowed you to convince me to turn from God.

You filled my heart with fearful thoughts. I was scared of my husband dying, afraid of my needs not being met, and afraid of God not hearing my prayers. Also, I was scared to trust Him, unsure if He forgave me for mistakes, scared to get to know the real me, feeling inadequate, not knowing where He wants me to be or do, not hearing or knowing God's voice afraid of rejection. You highlighted yourself in those circumstances I endured in my life. They had the most effect on the person I have become today. You just made it harder to dig down and find the gold within me.

Yes, you clogged my heart with all the negative emotions that positions God further away in my heart. But I'm grateful that I found my way back because eventually, I heard God's voice over yours. I lost value in myself, but everyone else could see it. You even saw my value; that's why you secretly came after me. Being a teen mom gave me some tough skin, fight, and determination. Being materialistic taught me that money is just a resource, not a source. Being unaware of who I really am showed me integrity, worth, and who I am—being impatient taught me how to respond to God and His timing, not mine. He knows what's best for me, but I allowed my anger and frustration of having my own agenda to cloud my judgments.

Not having a Bachelor's degree showed me that God has a plan for each one of us, individually. It also taught me to stay in my lane. Although God has promised every believer prosperity, we won't prosper the same way. So I didn't have to follow everybody's pattern. God has planned out my race for me, and there are instructions specific to me. For example, even if athletes have general meals they eat to keep fit, there are special menus specific to each athlete. I might love pork or seafood, whereas someone else might be allergic to it. No matter what someone does, he or she has to stay in their lane. So just accept that God's will for me is where I'm headed. I have tapped in and claiming my inheritance as God's daughter. Neither will I be envious of people who are successful because they followed their own path.

In fact, when you know too much, you try to be and do too much. God knew the path that He wanted me to take, and a BA would have taken me a different way. If He wants me to pursue that degree, I will know what to study when the time is right. Having low confidence showed me how low we can go inside and still have the endurance to get back up. Being angry showed me that life is less stressful if you allow God to have His way, and I won't be disappointed.

It's not always about me. Having some jealousy taught me that I enjoy helping others versus just watching what others do. If I'm busy helping someone, I don't have time to ponder what I wish I had when enjoying what I always wished for. It also taught me that I am my own competition. If I'm not happy where I am, then do something about it. Most times, that's an "inside job," not an "outside job." Little did you realize, you helped with my success; you gave me a story to tell and things to help others with. I still may run into you here and there, but I know you when I see you. I know how to play your game when you step into my arena. You are just an emotion. Going through struggles displays the power and ability that only God can give. This truth can be found in 2 Corinthians 12:9-10: *"And He said to me, "My grace is sufficient for you, for My strength is made perfect in weakness." Therefore most gladly I will rather boast in my infirmities, that the power of Christ may rest upon me. Therefore I take pleasure in infirmities, in reproaches, in needs, in persecutions, in distresses, for Christ's sake. For when I am weak, then I am strong."*

Scholars have different views about the weakness Paul wanted God to deal with. Some say that Paul had an eye defect. Well, no matter what it was, he cried to God to deliver him, and the reply was surprising. No doubt, he had believed God would alleviate his suffering. But you see, this suffering had a purpose. So, God wasn't quick to take it away but made him know that His grace was multiplied on account of his limitation.

I also experienced great suffering that wasn't extinguished when I desired it to end. That's when I met **Grace**. She showed me that forgiveness exists, and she brought **Mercy** with her. Mercy explained how she still looked out for me; it was always her role to do so. It became clear to me that God is with me every step of the way. It's just easier to detect Him when we have a relationship with Him. I was giving you all my relationships, talking, crying, and consulting with the wrong being. It was a funny situation because I made an alliance with the enemy and turned against God, who wanted to help me. But the truth is, no matter how hard you try, you can't alter God's purposes.

God makes everything work together for good in the lives of His children. A good example is Joseph. His brothers wanted to destroy his dream. They wanted his future to be bleak and without color. But the Bible reveals that what they meant for evil, God designed it to favor and enthroned him. Likewise, God used you to bless me. Certainly, your presence in my life was for evil, but the All-wise God used you as an instrument for my lifting. You even gave more ambition to the things that God wants to use me for. That's a weapon formed against me that won't prosper. I can now be proud of who I am and have become because of my shortcomings. I'm using those to my advantage.

You shielded me from talking to people but acting shy around those I didn't know, scared of having a microphone on a stage, and thinking outside of the box because those are things God wants me to use to reach and motivate His people. I thought that I would never reach a point in life where I can say, "I know why I'm here." **I'm here to be the one that you now fear!**

P.S. I think you misinterpreted your little fantasy dream in Chapter 3. See, I was myself, with the glow that only God can give me. That's why it was so impeccable. You were yourself, standing back and watching me because you saw something special about me. The ocean was my God-given purpose, endless like the ocean. The closer I got; the calmer things were. The farther I got, chaos would arise. As chaos was taking place, I could not hear you coming or feel you watching me. But when things chilled out, I was closer to my destiny which is closer to God. Likewise, the closer He is, the calmer things are for Him to hand you over your purpose and gifts. Once I recognized you were there, I chose to face you head-on during the chaos. But then I realized I didn't need to get closer because you could see in my eyes that I see you. I was smiling, thinking about all of your attempts to deter me from my calling, still didn't prosper.

Love,
    Me

"Drowning"

Have you ever felt as though you were drowning?

Drowning with hurt, confusion, insecurities, pain, delusion…

Maybe denial, rejection, *fears*.

Am I drowning in my tears?

Then suddenly, a whisper appears,

RISE!

Don't worry, I'll guide.

REVIVE!

Take heed and abide.

RELEASE!

Soar, never cease.

I whispered back, I thought you abandoned me.

He said, is that how it seemed?

But I planted you; I thought you knew…,

to produce something new.

And see, it was me

watering you, my seed.

Reminding you to grow,

blossoming with the glow.

Letting you know

I, your God, chose you to sow.

-Ebony White

Printed in Great Britain
by Amazon